from
the

APPLE
ORCHARD

recipes for apple lovers

A Collection of Recipes for Apple Lovers
Everywhere

by Lee Jackson

Cover, Illustrations and Calligraphy
by
Ione Pearson

FROM THE APPLE ORCHARD
Recipes for Apple Lovers

Published by

Images Unlimited
P.O. Box 305
Maryville, Missouri 64468

First Edition

First Printing — August, 1984
Second Printing — October, 1987
Third Printing — October, 1988
Fourth Printing — October, 1989
Fifth Printing — April, 1990
Sixth Printing — October, 1990
Seventh Printing — June, 1991
Eighth Printing — September, 1991
Ninth Printing — April, 1993
Tenth Printing — October, 1995

Printed in the United States of America

Rush Printing Company
Maryville, Missouri 64468

Other works by the author:

APPLES, APPLES EVERYWHERE
Favorite Recipes From America's Orchards

Library of Congress
Catalogue Card Number: 84-81309
ISBN 0-930643-00-3

Contents

Betty J.
Dzyk

From the apple orchard———

With thanks and appreciation to the many people who helped support and make this collection possible. To those who helped test recipes, I send my thanks—Mary Alice Cornelison, Marjory Barratt, Janet Scott, Roberta Richey, Karen Pfost, Marie Rash, Mildred Davis, Martha Sue Schrier, and Joan Mees.

To the faculty, administration and staff of Maryville R-II High School and Northwest Missouri State University, and our patient and loyal neighbors, for their many tasting sessions, I am appreciative of your kind words.

I especially wish to thank Ione Pearson, my good friend, for providing the art work and calligraphy for this endeavor, and to my husband, for his kind support and encouragement, despite the fact apples were on our menu in some form or another for many months on end.

I have always wanted an apple orchard, with its bountiful supply of sweet smelling fruit and beautiful apple blossoms. So, come with me, will you please, through this treasury of apple scented dishes, through my apple orchard. May these recipes bring joy and good eating to you and your family.

Lee Jackson

BEVERAGES

juice of the fruit

HOT CIDER

2 qts. cider or apple juice
1/2 cup brown sugar, firmly packed
1 stick cinnamon
6 whole cloves

In large saucepan, mix together cider or juice, sugar, and spices. Heat slowly to simmering. Cover pan and simmer 20 minutes. Strain out spices. Serve hot in heated mugs. Garnish with cinnamon sticks or orange wedges.

Yield: About 16 servings

*Come, gather around the fire
and sip the hot cider*

PERCULATOR MULLED CIDER

3 (46 oz.) cans apple juice
2 sticks cinnamon
6 whole cloves

In 30-cup coffee maker, pour the apple juice. In basket, place the cinnamon sticks, broken in pieces, and whole cloves. Perk through cycle of automatic coffee maker. Keep hot.

Yield: 24 servings

*Good for parties,
when you want to keep
the cider hot and handy*

HOT HOLLY CIDER

4 cups apple cider
4 cups cranberry juice cocktail
3 cinnamon sticks
6 whole cloves
Juice of 1/2 lemon
1/4 cup sugar

Mix all ingredients in a large pan and heat to boiling. Reduce heat and simmer 15 minutes. Remove spices before serving. Pour into pre-heated punch bowl. Float 2 or 3 small red apples, which have been studded with whole cloves.

Yield: 10-12 servings

The mulled, spicy aroma drifts deliciously through the house!

MULLED CIDER PUNCH

6   cups apple cider or juice
1   cinnamon stick
1/4   cup honey
1/4   tsp. nutmeg
Juice of 1   lemon
1   tsp. lemon peel
1   (18 oz.) can unsweetened pineapple juice

In large saucepan, heat cider or apple juice and cinnamon stick to boiling. Reduce heat. Cover. Simmer 5 minutes. Uncover and stir in remaining ingredients. Simmer 5 minutes longer. Serve hot in preheated punch bowl. Float orange slices on top of punch.

Yield: 12-16 servings

A favorite at holiday time

PERKY PUNCH

4 cups cider or apple juice
2 cups cranberry juice
1 cup orange juice
1/2 cup lemon juice
3/4 cup sugar
3 whole cloves
1 tsp. whole allspice
2 cinnamon sticks

Pour juices in 10-cup electric perculator. In basket, put the cloves, allspice, and cinnamon sticks. Perk through automatic cycle of coffee maker. Serve hot.

Yield: 12 servings

*A heavenly mulled, spicy
aroma permeates the air*

HOT CIDER PUNCH

8 cups apple cider
2 cups orange juice
1 cup lemon juice
1/4 cup honey
1 stick cinnamon
6 whole cloves
1/4 tsp. allspice
1 tsp. butter

Mix juices, honey, and spices together in large saucepan. Heat to simmering, cover, and gently simmer for 30 minutes. Add butter. Serve hot.

Yield: Approximately 16-20 servings

CIDER SHERBET PUNCH

2 qts. cider or apple juice, chilled
1 (10 oz.) bottle ginger ale
1 qt. lemon sherbet

Spoon sherbet into punch bowl. Pour cider or juice over the sherbet. Just before serving, add the ginger ale. If desired, garnish with sprigs of mint.

Yield: About 12 servings

FRUIT PUNCH

4 cups cider, or apple juice
2 cups orange juice
2 cups cranberry juice
1 bottle (28 oz.) ginger ale
1 qt. orange sherbet

Pour the chilled juices into punch bowl. Just before serving, pour in the ginger ale. Scoop mounds of sherbet on top. Garnish with sprigs of mint. Serve.

Yield: 16 servings

OPEN HOUSE PUNCH

4 qt. apple cider
2 cups orange juice
1/2 cup brown sugar
4 whole cloves
1 tsp. allspice
1/2 tsp. nutmeg

Rum to taste

Combine juices and brown sugar in large saucepan. Add spices and simmer gently for 30 minutes. Strain out whole cloves. Add rum, from 1/2 to whole bottle, just before serving. Can be served hot or cold.

Yield: 30 servings

CRAN-APPLE PUNCH

2 cups apple juice
2 cups cranberry juice
1 cup sugar
2 cups water
1 quart ginger ale

In large saucepan, boil together the sugar and water. Cool. Add chilled apple and cranberry juices. When ready to serve, pour in ginger ale.

Yield: About 20 servings

Festive and appropriate anytime

TANGY COOLER

1 qt. apple juice
1 can (6 oz.) frozen orange juice
1 can (6 oz.) frozen lemonade
2 qt. ginger ale

Thaw juices. Mix together the thawed juices, undiluted, and the apple juice. Add ginger ale just before serving.

Yield: 15, 7 oz. servings

FRUIT DRINK

1 (12 oz.) can frozen apple juice, reconstituted
1 (6 oz.) can frozen pineapple juice, reconstituted
1 orange, sliced

Thaw frozen juices and mix each as directed on can. Stir together and serve chilled in glasses with ice cubes. Garnish each glass with orange slice.

Yield: About 12 servings

APPLE ICED TEA

1/2 cup lemon-flavored iced tea mix
4 cups cold water
1 qt. apple juice
Ice cubes
1 lemon, sliced

In large pitcher, dissolve the iced tea mix in water. Stir in apple juice and tray of ice cubes. Pour in glasses and garnish with lemon slices.

Yield: About 8 servings

APPLE TANGY FIZZ

2 cups apple juice
2 cups ginger ale
1 pt. orange sherbet

Drop scoop of orange sherbet in each of 4 glasses. Pour juice and ginger ale over sherbet.

Yield: 4-6 servings

RUBY FIZZ

4 cups apple juice
2 cups cranberry juice cocktail
2 cups ginger ale

Chill juices and ginger ale. When ready to serve, add ginger ale to juices and pour into glasses. Garnish with lemon slice, if desired.

Yield: 8 servings

A hot weather refresher

APPLE SPICED TEA

1 (46 oz.) can apple juice
1 T. honey
4 whole cloves
1 stick cinnamon, broken in pieces
2 individual tea bags

In large saucepan, combine the juice, honey and spices. Bring mixture to a boil and turn off heat. Add the two tea bags, cover, and steep for 3 to 5 minutes. Take out tea bags and strain spices. Serve piping hot.

Yield: 6 to 8 servings

COLD BURGUNDY PUNCH

1   qt. cranberry-apple juice, chilled
2   cups Burgundy wine, chilled
3/4   cup sugar
1/2   cup water
1   stick cinnamon
4   whole cloves

In small saucepan, combine sugar, water, and the spices. Heat to boiling and then simmer for 10 minutes. Chill. Strain out the spices and combine with cranberry-apple juice and wine. Serve in a punch bowl or glass pitcher. Float small clove-studded apples.

Yield: Makes 12-4 oz. servings

HOT BURGUNDY APPLE PUNCH

2   cups apple juice or cider
1   cup orange juice
2   cups Burgundy wine
1   stick cinnamon
6   whole cloves
1/2   cup sugar
1/2   cup water
1   lemon, thinly sliced
1   orange, thinly sliced

Great for a get-together with friends after skiing or whatever

Combine sugar, water, and spices in medium saucepan. Heat to a boil, then simmer gently 5 minutes, until sugar dissolves. Add the apple juice and orange juice and heat, but do not boil. Just before serving, add the wine. Reheat. Strain out the spices. Pour into preheated punch bowl. Float thin orange and lemon slices in punch.

Yield: About 10-12 servings

APPLE AND CIDER DAIQUIRI

1 medium apple, unpeeled, cored
3 oz. apple cider
3 oz. light rum
3 oz. prepared limeade made from frozen concentrate,
   or juice of one lime
2 tsp. sugar
2 cups crushed ice

Chop apple. Place all ingredients in blender and blend on slow to medium speed for 20-30 seconds, or until nearly frozen. Pour into glasses. Garnish with apple slices which have been dipped in lime juice.

Yield: 2 servings

APPLEJACK AND CIDER

3 oz. apple cider
3 oz. applejack
Dash of dry vermouth
Ice
Lemon slice

Pour 1/2 of the cider and applejack over ice in each of two glasses. Add a dash of dry vermouth to each glass. Cut lemon slice in half and lightly squeeze each half in glass. Stir.

Yield: 2 servings

APPETIZERS

good seeds  *for starters*

FRUIT AND CHEESE APPETIZERS

On serving tray, alternate slices of unpeeled apples, which have been dipped in lemon or pineapple juice, with various cheeses. Some cheese suggestions are:
1) Blue
2) Camembert
3) Cheddar
4) Monterray Jack
5) Swiss

Add a wine for entertaining late-night guests

APPLE TRAY APPETIZERS

Apple dip

3 oz. cream cheese
2 T. milk
1 tsp. crumbled blue cheese

Whip ingredients together until soft and of "dipping" consistency. On small plate, arrange in a circle, sliced, unpeeled apples which have been dipped in lemon juice or pineapple juice. Insert toothpicks in each apple slice. Have dip in small dish in center of plate.

Another dip suggestion:
1 (5 oz.) jar cream cheese with pineapple
2 T. dairy sour cream

Whip together until of desired consistency.

Delicious, & very attractive

SNACK SPREAD

2 tart apples, peeled and finely chopped
2 slices bacon, fried crisp
3 oz. cream cheese
2 T. milk
1 T. blue cheese dressing
1/4 tsp. Worcestershire sauce
Dash of paprika

Assorted snack crackers

Gradually add milk to softened cream cheese. Blend in blue cheese dressing and Worcestershire sauce. Stir in apples. Crumble in crisp bacon. Refrigerate to blend flavors. When ready to serve, sprinkle with paprika. Serve with crackers.

Yield: About 1 cup

*Just a hint of blue cheese,
use up the same day*

FRUIT SPARKLE

4 Delicious apples
1 (11 oz.) can mandarin oranges
4 maraschino cherries, halved
2 cups ginger ale, chilled

Slice unpeeled apples into sections. Combine with drained mandarin oranges in individual dishes. Pour chilled ginger ale over fruit. Top with maraschino cherries.

Yield: 6-8 servings

*Makes a refreshing first
course or quick dessert*

ACCOMPANIMENTS

branching ~ out - - -

FRIED APPLES

4 cooking apples
4 T. butter or margarine
1/3 cup brown sugar

Core apples and cut into rings, but do not peel. Melt butter in skillet. Add brown sugar, then apple rings. Cook apples slowly, turning carefully with spatula to keep from burning. Cook until transparent and tender, but will still hold their shape.

Yield: 4 servings

GLAZED APPLES

6 apples, unpeeled, quartered, and cored
3/4 cup sugar
1 T. butter or margarine
3 T. water

In skillet, melt butter and add sugar and water. Place apples in skillet. Cover and cook slowly until a golden brown.

Yield: 4 servings

*Great as a ham or roast
turkey accompaniment*

APPLE-SAUSAGE-RICE DRESSING

8   oz. mild pork sausage
1/2   cup chopped onion
1/2   cup chopped celery
1   cup uncooked rice
1   (8 oz.) can water chestnuts, drained
2   cups beef broth

2   tart cooking apples, coarsely chopped
1/4   cup slivered almonds, toasted

Brown crumbled sausage in large, heavy skillet. Sauté onions last few minutes. Add celery and cook until tender. Add rice, water chestnuts, and beef broth. Bring to a boil; cover.

Bake at 350° for 30 minutes, or until liquid is absorbed. Remove from oven and stir in apples. Cover and let stand few minutes. Sprinkle with slivered almonds before serving.

Yield: 8-10 servings

*Serve with ham, or steam a green
vegetable & serve this as the main course*

APPLE HORSERADISH SAUCE

1   cup applesauce
2   tsp. prepared horseradish
1/4   tsp. salt

Combine ingredients and chill.

Yield: 1 cup

*Tangy meat sauce, especially
for ham loaf & pork roast*

CASSEROLE APPLES

5-6   large cooking apples
2   T. lemon juice
1/2#   peanut brittle, crushed fine

Peel and slice cooking apples. Place in buttered 2 qt. casserole. Sprinkle lemon juice and peanut brittle over top. Bake in 325° oven for 45-60 minutes.

Yield: 8 servings

APPLE FRITTERS

1 egg
3/4 cup milk
1/2 tsp. vanilla
1 cup flour
2 tsp. baking powder
2 T. sugar
1/2 tsp. salt
4 cooking apples

2 T. sugar
1/2 tsp. cinnamon

Confectioners' sugar

To make batter, beat egg, add milk and vanilla. Mix in dry ingredients and beat just until smooth. Peel and core apples. Slice in 1/4" rings. Dip rings in batter and drop into skillet containing 1/2" hot grease. Fry until golden brown, turning once. Drain on absorbent paper.

Mix cinnamon and sugar and sprinkle over fritters, or roll in confectioners' sugar. Serve at once.

Yield: 16-20 fritters

BAKED APPLES

4 cooking apples
1/4 cup granulated sugar
4 tsp. brown sugar
2 tsp. butter or margarine
1/4 tsp. cinnamon
1/8 tsp. nutmeg
1/2 cup water

Core apples, but not all the way through. Place apples in 8"
x 11" baking pan. In each cavity put 1 T. granulated sugar and
1 tsp. brown sugar. Top with 1/2 tsp. butter or margarine.
Sprinkle with cinnamon and nutmeg. Pour 1/2 cup water around
apples. Bake at 350° for 30-40 minutes, or until apples are tender
but still hold shape.

Yield: 4 servings

CURRIED HOT FRUIT

1 (16 oz.) can peach halves
1 (16 oz.) can pear halves
1 (16 oz.) can apricot halves
1 (8 oz.) can pineapple chunks
4 baking apples, peeled and sliced
Juice of 1 lemon
1/2 tsp. nutmeg
1/2 tsp. cinnamon
1/4 tsp. ground cloves
1/3 cup butter or margarine
1/3 cup brown sugar
1 tsp. curry powder
4 maraschino cherries, with stems

Drain canned fruit. Mix together the juices and reserve 1 1/2 cups. Arrange canned fruits in 2 qt. baking dish. Coat sliced apples with lemon juice and add to the fruit. In a saucepan, melt the butter or margarine, add brown sugar, spices, and the reserved syrup. Heat at low temperature, stirring to blend. Spoon over fruit. Bake in 350° oven for 25 minutes. Garnish with cherries.

Yield: 10-12 servings

Excellent as a meat accompaniment

SALADS

colorful & crunchy

BERRY-APPLE SALAD

1 (3 oz.) pkg. raspberry gelatin
1 cup hot water
1 (10 oz.) pkg. frozen raspberries
1 cup thick applesauce

Dissolve gelatin in hot water. Add raspberries, stirring until thawed; add the applesauce. Pour into 9" square pan. Refrigerate until firm. Spread on topping:

Topping

1 (3 oz.) pkg. cream cheese
1 cup miniature marshmallows
1 cup whipped topping

Soften cream cheese until it can be easily mixed into the whipped topping. Add marshmallows. Spread on top of jellied salad.

Yield: 9-12 servings

Served this at a graduation buffet—colorful & good

RUBY SALAD

1   (1#) pkg. fresh cranberries
2   cups sugar
1   cup water
1   pkg. strawberry gelatin
1/2   pkg. marshmallows, or about 20
2   apples, peeled and diced

Cook cranberries, sugar, and water over medium heat until cranberries have popped and are cooked. Remove from heat, add gelatin and stir until dissolved. Add the marshmallows and stir until they are melted. Let cool, then stir in the apples and chill until set.

Yield: 12 servings

Remember this recipe when it's cranberry season!

APPLE WALDORF MOLD

1   (3 oz.) pkg. lemon gelatin
1/2   cup boiling water
1   cup apple cider or ginger ale
1   red apple, unpeeled and diced
1   stalk celery, diced
1/4   cup halved, seedless white grapes
1   banana, peeled and sliced
4   maraschino cherries

Dissolve gelatin in hot water. Add apple cider or ginger ale. Chill until partially thickened. Combine apples, celery, grapes, and maraschino cherries and fold into gelatin mixture. Pour into mold. Chill until set. Unmold on lettuce lined plate.

Yield: 6-8 servings

A nice variation of the Waldorf salad

SPARKLING CRAN-APPLE SALAD

1   (3 oz.) pkg. raspberry gelatin
1   cup boiling water
1   (1#) can jellied cranberry sauce
1   cup apples, unpeeled, chopped
1/2   cup chopped nuts

Dissolve gelatin in boiling water. Stir in cranberry sauce, using a fork or whip to break up the lumps. Chill until slightly thickened, then add the apples and nuts. Chill until set, 2-3 hours.

Yield: 8 servings

Just excellent!

FROZEN SALAD

1 (8 1/4 oz.) can pineapple tidbits, in own juice
2 eggs, beaten
1/3 cup sugar
1 T. lemon juice
3 medium red Delicious apples, unpeeled, diced
1 cup whipped topping

Drain pineapple and reserve the juice. Measure juice and add water to equal 1/2 cup. In saucepan, add juice, beaten eggs, sugar, and lemon juice. Cook until thickened, stirring constantly. Cool.

Stir in apples and pineapple tidbits. Gently fold in whipped topping. Pour into a 9" x 9" pan and freeze. Take out of freezer 1/2 hour before serving and cut into squares. Serve on bed of lettuce. Garnish with maraschino cherries, if desired.

Yield: 9-12 servings

*High school foods class
served this at a dinner —
very successful*

THREE-FRUIT SALAD

1 red Delicious apple, unpeeled, cut in small pieces
1 banana, peeled and sliced
1/4 cup pineapple chunks, drained

Combine fruit and serve with following dressing:

Dressing

1/4 cup plain yogurt
1 T. pineapple juice
1 tsp. sugar
1/8 tsp. nutmeg

Blend ingredients and pour over fruit. Serve fruit salad on bed of lettuce.

Yield: 4 servings

Also, try apples, oranges & avocados or ?,
Be original, Be creative with apples,

FRUIT SALAD BOWL

2   apples, unpeeled, diced
1   (8 oz.) can crushed pineapple, drained
1   cup cheddar cheese, diced

1   tsp. mayonnaise
1/4   cup sour cream
1   tsp. lemon juice
1   tsp. sugar
Dash of salt

Core and dice apples. Add drained pineapple and diced cheese. Combine mayonnaise, sour cream, lemon juice, sugar, and salt. Mix together lightly in bowl; chill. Serve.

Yield: 4 servings

Apples & cheese – delightfully pared !

SPECIAL APPLE WALDORF SALAD

2   medium red apples, unpeeled, cubed
1   stalk celery, diced
1   can (8 1/4 oz.) pineapple chunks, drained
1/4   cup miniature marshmallows
1/4—1/2   cup mayonnaise or salad dressing
1   T. sugar
1   T. milk

1/2   cup shredded cheese

Combine mayonnaise or salad dressing, milk and sugar in small bowl. Pour this mixture over the cut-up apples, diced celery, and pineapple chunks. Serve on lettuce leaf. Sprinkle top with shredded cheese.

Yield: 4 servings

Colorful & good

APPLE CABBAGE SALAD

1/2 medium size head cabbage
2 red apples, unpeeled
1 stalk celery

Shred cabbage and add chopped apples and diced celery. Pour dressing over this.

Dressing

2 T. sugar
2 T. flour
2 T. water
·3 T. cider vinegar
1/2 tsp. salt
1/8 tsp. pepper
2 T. butter or margarine
1 egg

In top of double boiler, combine all ingredients except egg. Cook until slightly thickened, then pour small amount of mixture into beaten egg. Continue cooking for five minutes, stirring constantly. Cool. Thin with milk, if necessary.

Yield: 4-6 servings

Tasty cabbage salad - with a good home-prepared dressing

CRAN-APPLE-MALLOW SALAD

1 # raw cranberries, ground
1 # miniature marshmallows
1 cup sugar
2 cups apples, peeled and diced
1/2 cup seedless grapes
2 cups whipped topping

Grind raw cranberries. Combine ground cranberries, marshmallows, and sugar. Refrigerate several hours and then add the apples and grapes. Fold in whipped topping. Chill or freeze.

Yield: 8-10 servings

Another recipe for the fresh cranberry season

AUTUMN FRUIT SALAD

1   red apple, unpeeled and cut up
1   banana, sliced
1   cup seedless grapes
1/2   cup shredded cheese

Lettuce

Dressing

1   T. honey
1   T. red wine vinegar
3   T. vegetable oil
1/4   tsp. dry mustard

Cut up fruit and place in lettuce lined salad bowls. Drizzle dressing over top. Sprinkle with shredded cheese.

Yield: 4 servings

*Dressing is especially good -
& the shredded cheese adds the winning touch*

BREADS

hybread varieties

CINNAMON TOPPED MUFFINS

1 1/2 cups flour
2 tsp. baking powder
1/2 tsp. salt
1/2 tsp. cinnamon
1/2 tsp. nutmeg
1/4 tsp. cloves
3/4 cup sugar
1/3 cup shortening
1 egg, well beaten
1/2 cup milk
2 tart apples, peeled and chopped

Sift together dry ingredients. Cream sugar and shortening. Add beaten egg. Stir in dry ingredients alternately with the milk. Stir only until flour is moistened. Gently fold in apples. Spoon into well-greased muffin tins and fill 2/3. Sprinkle top with cinnamon mixture. Bake at 425° for 20-25 minutes.

Cinnamon mixture

2 T. sugar
1/2 tsp. cinnamon

Yield: 1 dozen muffins

Always serve muffins piping hot!

APPLE MUFFINS

2 cups flour
3 tsp. baking powder
1/2 tsp. salt
1/2 tsp. cinnamon
1/2 tsp. nutmeg
1/4 cup sugar
1 cup milk
1 egg, well beaten
3 T. vegetable oil
1 cup grated raw apple
1/4 cup walnuts

Sift together dry ingredients. Combine egg, milk, and oil in mixing bowl. Add dry ingredients. Mix only enough to moisten. Fold in apples and nuts. Fill greased muffin tins 2/3 full. Bake at 375° for 20-25 minutes.

Yield: 12 muffins

Mix muffins quickly & lightly

GOOD MORNING MUFFINS

1 1/2 cups flour
1 1/2 tsp. baking powder
1/2 tsp. salt
1/2 tsp. nutmeg
1/2 cup sugar
1/3 cup shortening
1 egg
1 tsp. vanilla
1/2 cup milk
1 cup apples, peeled and grated
1/2 cup walnuts

2 T. butter or margarine, melted
2 T. sugar
1/4 tsp. cinnamon

Cream sugar and shortening. Add egg, vanilla, milk, and grated apples. Sift together dry ingredients and add all at once. Mix only until blended. Fold in walnuts. Spoon into well-greased muffin tins. Fill 2/3 full.

Bake in 350° oven for 20-25 minutes. When baked, remove from pan and roll muffins in melted butter, then dip tops into sugar-cinnamon mixture. Serve hot.

Yield: 12 muffins

If any are left over, they freeze beautifully,
To reheat frozen muffins, unwrap & bake
at 350° for 10 minutes,

STREUSEL FILLED APPLE MUFFINS

1 1/2 cups flour
2 tsp. baking powder
1/4 cup sugar
1/2 tsp. nutmeg
1/4 cup vegetable oil
1 egg, beaten
1/2 cup milk
1 medium apple, peeled and grated

Sift together dry ingredients. Make a well and pour in oil, milk, beaten egg, and grated apples. Mix only until moistened. Spoon 3/4 of batter into well-greased muffin tins. Sprinkle streusel filling over each, then top with 1 tsp. batter. Bake at 350° for 20-25 minutes.

Streusel Filling

1/4 cup brown sugar
1 T. flour
1/2 tsp. cinnamon
1 T. butter or margarine, melted
1/4 cup chopped nuts

Yield: 1 dozen muffins

APPLE-CHEESE LOAF

2 1/2 cups flour
2 tsp. baking powder
1/2 tsp. salt
3/4 tsp. cinnamon
1/2 tsp. nutmeg
1/2 cup sugar
1/4 cup vegetable oil
2 eggs
3/4 cup milk
1 1/2 cups apples, peeled and chopped
1/4 cup nuts, chopped
2 cups (8 oz.) shredded cheddar cheese

Sift together dry ingredients into bowl. Make a well and add oil, eggs, and milk. Mix only until blended. Fold in chopped apples, nuts and cheese. Pour into well-greased 9" x 5" x 3" loaf pan. Bake at 350° for 60-70 minutes.

Yield: 1 large loaf

This is a very tasty & delicious quick bread.

EARLY AMERICAN APPLESAUCE BREAD

2 cups flour
2 tsp. baking powder
1 tsp. baking soda
1 tsp. cinnamon
1/2 tsp. nutmeg
3/4 cup sugar
1/2 cup shortening
1 tsp. vanilla
2 eggs
1 cup unsweetened applesauce

Sift together dry ingredients. Cream sugar and shortening. Add vanilla. Blend in eggs, beating well after each. Add dry ingredients. Stir in applesauce. Pour into a greased 9" x 5" x 3" loaf pan. Sprinkle topping over batter, then bake at 350° for 55-60 minutes.

Topping

1/4 cup flour
1/2 cup brown sugar
2 T. butter or margarine, softened
1/2 tsp. cinnamon
1/4 cup chopped nuts

Yield: 1 large loaf

SPICED APPLE LOAF

3 cups flour
1 tsp. baking powder
1 tsp. baking soda
1/2 tsp. salt
1 tsp. cinnamon
1/2 tsp. nutmeg
1 1/2 cups sugar
3 eggs
1/2 cup vegetable oil
1/2 cup sour milk
2 cups apples, peeled and grated
1/2 cup chopped nuts
1 tsp. vanilla

In large mixing bowl, sift the dry ingredients and mix together. Make a well in the center and add eggs, oil, and sour milk. Mix well. Blend in apples, nuts, and vanilla.

Pour batter into 2 greased 9" x 5" x 3" loaf pans and bake at 325° for 55-60 minutes. Remove from pans and cool on rack.

Yield: 2 loaves

Bake one loaf for yourself & give one away.

APPLE-BANANA LOAF

3/4 cup sugar
1/4 cup shortening
2 eggs
1/4 cup milk
2 cups flour
2 tsp. baking powder
1 tsp. baking soda
1/2 tsp. salt
2 cups apples, grated
1 ripe banana, mashed
1/4 cup nuts, chopped

Cream together sugar and shortening. Beat in eggs. Add milk and stir. Sift together dry ingredients and stir into creamed mixture. Fold in apples and banana and nuts.

Bake in greased 9" x 5" x 3" loaf pan at 350° for 50-60 minutes.

Yield: 1 large loaf

Good way to use that one last, very ripe banana

APPLESAUCE LOAF BREAD

2 cups flour
3/4 cup sugar
3 tsp. baking powder
1/2 tsp. baking soda
1 tsp. salt
1 egg
1/4 cup butter or margarine, melted
1 cup canned applesauce
1/2 tsp. cinnamon
1/2 cup nuts, chopped

In mixing bowl, beat egg slightly. Add melted butter and applesauce. Add dry ingredients and nuts. Stir only until blended. Spoon into well-greased 9" x 5" x 3" loaf pan and bake at 350° for 60 minutes. Can also be baked in 2 8" x 3" x 2" pans at 350° for 40-45 minutes.

Yield: 1 large loaf or 2 smaller loaves

SPICY APPLESAUCE QUICK BREAD

3   cups flour
2   tsp. baking powder
1   tsp. baking soda
1   tsp. salt
1/2   cup granulated sugar
1/2   cup brown sugar, firmly packed
1/2   tsp. cinnamon
1/2   tsp. nutmeg
1/4   tsp. allspice
2   eggs
1/2   cup vegetable oil
1 1/2   cups applesauce
1   tsp. vanilla
1   cup nuts, chopped

Stir together dry ingredients in large mixing bowl. Make a well and add eggs, oil, applesauce and vanilla. Stir just until blended. Fold in nuts. Pour into a greased 9" x 5" x 3" loaf pan and bake at 350° for 60-70 minutes. Let cool 10 minutes. Remove from pan and cool completely before slicing.

Yield: 1   9"x5"x3" loaf or 2   8"x3"x2" loaves

Spread with cream cheese for a delicious break

QUICK APPLESAUCE BREAD

2 cups flour
1 1/2 tsp. baking powder
1 tsp. baking soda
1/2 cup shortening
2/3 cup brown sugar
2 eggs
1 tsp. vanilla
1 cup applesauce
1/4 cup nuts, chopped

Heat applesauce until warm. Cream together shortening and brown sugar. Add eggs and mix well. Blend in vanilla. Stir in dry ingredients, except baking soda. Add the soda to the heated applesauce and quickly stir into batter. Add nuts. Spoon into a well-greased 9" x 5" x 3" loaf pan. Bake at 350° for 55-65 minutes.

Yield: 1 loaf

APPLE HONEY COFFEE CAKE

2/3 cup sugar
1/4 cup shortening
1 egg
1/2 cup milk
1 1/2 cups flour
2 tsp. baking powder
1/4 tsp. salt
1/4 tsp. cinnamon
1/8 tsp. nutmeg
2 medium apples, peeled and sliced

Cream sugar and shortening. Add egg and mix until fluffy. Gradually stir in milk with the sifted dry ingredients. Spread in a well greased 8" round cake pan. Arrange apple slices over top. Sprinkle crumb mixture over apples. Drizzle topping over all. Bake at 375° for 35-40 minutes.

Crumb Mixture

1/3 cup brown sugar
2 T. flour
1/2 tsp. cinnamon
3 T. butter, cut in

Topping

2 T. butter, melted
3 T. honey
1/2 cup nuts, chopped

Yield: *8 servings*

APPLE BISCUIT COFFEE CAKE

2   cooking apples, peeled and sliced
2   T. butter or margarine
1/4   cup raisins
1   can refrigerated ready-to-bake biscuits

1/4   cup brown sugar
1/2   tsp. cinnamon
1/4   cup light corn syrup
1   egg
1/4   cup walnuts
1 T.   butter or margarine

Melt 2 T. of butter in bottom of 9" round cake pan. Arrange sliced apples over butter. Sprinkle raisins over apples. Cut each of the 10 biscuits into fourths and place over apples.

Mix together the brown sugar, cinnamon, corn syrup and egg until well blended and sugar is dissolved. Pour over biscuits. Sprinkle walnuts over top. Dot with 1 T. butter.

Bake at 350° for 35-45 minutes. Invert on serving plate, spooning juices over top.

Yield: 6-8 servings

This is the recipe to make for Sunday morning breakfast, easy & good!

AUTUMN COFFEE CAKE

1 cup sugar
1/2 cup shortening
2 eggs
1 tsp. vanilla
2 cups flour
1 tsp. baking powder
1 tsp. baking soda
1/2 tsp. salt
1 cup sour cream
2 cups apples, peeled and chopped

Cream together shortening and sugar. Add eggs and vanilla. Beat well. Add sour cream and dry ingredients; mix well. Fold in apples. Spread in greased 9" x 13" pan. Sprinkle topping over batter.

Topping

2 T. butter or margarine, melted
1/2 cup brown sugar
1/4 cup nuts

Blend together butter and brown sugar. Add nuts. Sprinkle over coffee cake batter. Bake at 350° for 30-35 minutes.

Yield: 9-12 servings

APPLE STREUSEL COFFEE CAKE

2 1/2 cups flour
2 cups brown sugar
1/2 tsp. salt
2/3 cup butter or margarine, softened

Mix all together until well combined, but crumbly. Reserve 1/2 cup mixture for topping. To remaining crumb mixture add:

2 tsp. baking powder
1/2 tsp. soda
1/2 tsp. cinnamon
1/4 tsp. nutmeg
1 cup sour milk
2 eggs, beaten
1 tart apple, peeled and diced

Mix well. Pour into greased 9" x 13" pan. Sprinkle reserved crumb mixture over top. Bake at 350° for 35-40 minutes.

Yield: 9-12 servings

WALNUT APPLE COFFEE CAKE

1   cup brown sugar
1/2   cup shortening
1   egg, beaten
1 1/2   cups flour
1   tsp. soda
1/2   tsp. cinnamon
1/4   tsp. salt
2   cups apples, peeled and chopped

Cream thoroughly brown sugar and shortening. Add beaten egg. Sift together dry ingredients and add to creamed mixture. Blend in 2 cups peeled and chopped apples. Pour into 9" square greased pan. Sprinkle topping on batter.

Topping

2   T. butter or margarine
1/2   cup brown sugar
1/2   cup walnuts, chopped
1   tsp. cinnamon

Blend brown sugar and butter. Mixture will be lumpy. Add walnuts and cinnamon. Sprinkle on top of batter.
Bake at 350° for 30-35 minutes.

Yield: 6-8 servings

Sure to get 'apple-awes'!

APPLE COFFEE CAKE

1   cup flour
2   tsp. baking powder
1/2   tsp. salt
1/2   cup sugar
1/2   cup milk
1   egg
1/3   cup shortening, melted
1   cup quick cooking oats
3   large cooking apples, peeled and sliced

Beat egg, add milk and melted shortening. Sift together dry ingredients and add to liquid. Stir in oats. Pour half of batter into a greased 9" x 9" baking pan. Slice apples over batter and sprinkle with 1/2 of topping. Pour remaining batter over apples. Sprinkle with remaining topping. Bake at 375° for 30 minutes, or until done.

Topping

1/2   cup brown sugar
1/2   tsp. cinnamon
1/4   tsp. nutmeg
2   T. butter or margarine, melted

Mix brown sugar, cinnamon and nutmeg. Mix in melted butter.

Yield: 9 servings

APPLE AND OATS YEAST BREAD

2 pkg. yeast
1/4 cup warm water
1 1/2 cups milk, scalded
1/4 cup sugar
2 tsp. salt
1/4 cup shortening
2 eggs
4 1/2—5 1/2 cups flour
1 1/2 cups rolled oats

1 cup apples, peeled and sliced

2 T. melted butter or margarine
6 T. brown sugar
1 tsp. cinnamon

Scald milk. Add shortening and stir to dissolve. Add rolled oats to mixture. Cool to lukewarm. Dissolve yeast in warm water, add sugar and salt. Pour in lukewarm milk mixture. Stir in 1 cup flour and 2 eggs. Beat vigorously. Gradually stir in enough of remaining flour to make a soft dough. Turn out on lightly floured board and knead about 10 minutes. Place in a greased bowl, turning once to grease top. Cover and let rise in warm place until doubled in bulk, about 1 hour.

Punch down. Divide dough in half and roll each half into a rectangle 8" x 15". Brush each rectangle with 1 T. melted butter, 3 T. of brown sugar, and 1/2 tsp. cinnamon. Over this, arrange 1/2 cup sliced apples. Roll up as for jelly roll. Place in 2 greased 9" x 5" x 3" loaf pans. Let rise until double, about an hour.

Bake at 375° for 40-45 minutes. Brush tops with butter. Cool out of pans.

Yield: 2 loaves

A very tender, delicious product

APPLE YEAST BREAD

1 pkg. dry yeast
1/4 cup warm water
3/4 cup milk, scalded
1/4 cup sugar
1/4 cup shortening
1 tsp. salt
2 eggs, beaten
3-4 1/2 cups flour
2 cooking apples

2 T. butter or margarine, melted
2 T. sugar
1/4 tsp. cinnamon

Scald milk, add shortening, sugar and salt, stirring until shortening melts. Cool to lukewarm. Dissolve yeast in warm water, then add cooled milk mixture. Stir in beaten eggs. Beat in 2 cups flour until smooth. Add enough of the remaining flour to handle easily. Knead until smooth and elastic (about 5 minutes). Place in a greased bowl, turning to grease top. Cover and let rise in warm place until double in bulk (about 1 hour). Punch down and divide into two parts. Shape and place in 2 greased 9" x 5" x 3" bread pans.

Cut peeled apples into slices. Press into top of dough. Brush tops of dough with melted butter. Combine sugar and cinnamon. Sprinkle mixture lightly over apples. Cover. Let rise in warm place until doubled in size. Bake at 350° for 40-50 minutes, or until a golden brown. Remove immediately from pans and let cool. When cool, frost with confectioners' sugar icing.

1 1/2 cups confectioners' sugar
2 T. milk
1 tsp. vanilla

Yield: 2 large loaves

HOME BAKED APPLE TURNOVERS

1 can prepared apple pie filling

Dough

1/2 cup milk
1/3 cup sugar
1 1/2 tsp. salt
1/4 cup shortening
1/2 cup warm water
2 pkg. yeast
2 eggs, beaten
3 1/2—4 1/2 cups flour

      In large bowl, dissolve yeast in warm water. Heat milk; stir in shortening, sugar and salt. Cool to lukewarm and add to yeast. Add beaten eggs and half of flour. Beat until smooth and elastic. Stir in rest of flour to make a soft dough. Knead until smooth-about 10 minutes. Place in greased bowl. Cover and let rise until doubled.

      Punch down and divide into 3 sections. Roll out each ball to 8" x 11" and cut into squares. Add a tablespoon of prepared pie filling to each square. Place on greased cookie sheet and fold over into rectangle or triangle. Seal edges by pressing down. Cut few slashes in each turnover.

      Bake immediately at 375° for 15-20 minutes. If desired, drizzle confectioners' sugar icing over turnovers when cool.

Yield: 24 turnovers

KOLACHE

Dough for bottom crust:

1 pkg. dry yeast
2/3 cup warm water
2/3 cup warm milk
2 T. sugar
2 tsp. salt
1/4 cup shortening
3 1/2—4 cups flour

In large mixing bowl, dissolve yeast in lukewarm water. Heat milk, add sugar, salt, and shortening, cool to lukewarm. Add to yeast mixture in bowl. Stir in 1/2 of the flour and beat until smooth. Gradually add more of the flour to make a soft dough. Turn out on board and knead until smooth and satiny. Place in greased bowl, cover, and let rise until double in bulk. Punch down. Divide dough in fourths. Grease bottom and sides of 4 pie pans. Roll out each ball the size of bottom of pie pan. Let rise 20-30 minutes. Press dough down slightly to keep a higher ridge around outside. Fill center with apple filling, or other filling, and bake immediately.

Apple Filling

3 medium apples, peeled and sliced
1/3 cup sugar
1/2 tsp. cinnamon
1/2 cup graham cracker crumbs
2 T. butter or margarine, melted

Lightly toss apples with sugar and cinnamon. Arrange apples on top of dough in each pan, cover to edge, leaving a narrow ridge. Sprinkle 1/2 of the graham cracker crumbs on top. Drizzle 1 T. of melted butter over top of each kolache. Makes enough for 2 kolaches.

Bake immediately in 400° oven for 12-15 minutes. Brush crust with melted butter and drizzle a teaspoon of melted butter over each kolache. Cut into 6 pie shaped servings. Eat in hand or with a fork.

Apple-Butter Filling

5 apples, peeled and sliced
3/4 cup sugar
1/2 tsp. cinnamon
1/2 cup water

1/4 cup graham cracker crumbs
2 T. butter or margarine, melted

Cook apples in sugar, cinnamon and water until very tender. Put through sieve. Cool. After filling is spread on kolache, sprinkle with the graham cracker crumbs and drizzle butter over top. Makes enough for 2 kolaches.

Prune-Applesauce Filling

1 1/2 cups dried prunes
3/4 cup sugar
1/2 cup applesauce

Cover prunes with water and cook until tender. Remove pits. Chop prunes and add sugar. Mix in applesauce. Use as filling for kolache. Makes enough for 2 kolaches.

*Included as a tribute
to a Czech heritage*

APPLE STYLE YEAST DOUGHNUTS

1 pkg. dry yeast
1 tsp. sugar
3/4 cup milk, scalded
2 cups flour
3 T. sugar
1/2 tsp. salt
2 eggs
1 cup apples, peeled and chopped
2 T. mixed candied fruit
Cooking oil
Confectioners' sugar

Scald milk; cool to lukewarm. Sprinkle yeast over milk, add sugar and stir to dissolve. Sift dry ingredients into a bowl. Make a well in center and pour in yeast and milk mixture and eggs. Beat thoroughly. Stir in apples and candied fruit. Cover. Let rise in a warm place until doubled in bulk, about 1 hour.

Into deep hot oil (350°) drop heaping tablespoons of the batter and fry until golden brown (about 3 minutes). Drain and dust with confectioners' sugar.

Yield: 21 doughnuts

SPICY APPLESAUCE DOUGHNUTS

1/4 cup shortening
1 cup sugar
3 eggs
1 tsp. vanilla
1 cup applesauce
5-6 cups flour
4 tsp. baking powder
1 tsp. baking soda
1 1/2 tsp. salt
1 tsp. cinnamon
1 tsp. nutmeg
1/4 tsp. allspice
1/2 cup buttermilk

Cream shortening and sugar. Add eggs and beat well. Blend in vanilla and applesauce. Sift dry ingredients and mix in gradually with the buttermilk, beginning and ending with the flour. Add enough flour to form a soft dough. Pat out to 1/2" thickness on a floured board. Cut into doughnut shapes and drop in deep fat (375°) until golden brown. Dust with sugar, if desired.

Yield: 2 dozen doughnuts + holes

MICROWAVE APPLE PANCAKES

3 T. butter or margarine
2 medium cooking apples, peeled and sliced
1/3 cup sugar
1/4 tsp. cinnamon
1/4 tsp. allspice

Pancake Batter

1 cup pancake mix
3/4 cup water

In glass 9" pie pan, melt butter in microwave. Mix in sliced apples, sugar, and spices. Cover. Microwave until apples are tender (3-4 minutes).

Mix together pancake batter and pour over apples in pie pan. Microwave until a toothpick inserted 2" from edge comes out clean (about 3-5 minutes). Let stand few minutes, then invert on serving plate. Cut into 6 pieces. Serve.

Yield: 6 servings

APPLE FOLD OVERS

3-4 tart apples
2 T. butter or margarine
1/4 cup sugar
1/4 tsp. cinnamon
1/8 tsp. nutmeg

Prepare apple filling by peeling apples and slicing thin. In 10" ovenproof skillet, sauté apples for 5 minutes in butter. Sprinkle sugar and spices over apples. Cover and continue cooking for 10 minutes. Spoon into another dish.

Batter

2 eggs
1/2 cup milk
1/2 cup flour
1 T. sugar
1/4 tsp. salt
1 T. butter or margarine

Beat eggs with rotary beater. Add milk and dry ingredients. Beat until smooth. Melt 1 T. butter in 10" ovenproof skillet. Pour in batter. Bake in 450° oven for 10 minutes. When batter puffs up in center, puncture with fork, repeating if necessary. Lower temperature to 350 ° and continue baking for 10 minutes. Remove from oven. Spread apple filling over one-half of the mixture. Fold over. Place on serving plate. Sprinkle confectioners' sugar over top.

Yield: 4-6 servings

Good for breakfast as a glorified pancake or as a delectable dessert

APPLE PANCAKES

2 cups pancake mix
1 tsp. sugar
1/4 tsp. cinnamon
2 medium apples, peeled and chopped fine
1 cup milk
1 egg
1 T. vegetable oil

Mix sugar and cinnamon into pancake mix. Stir in apples and add milk, egg, and oil. Bake on a hot, heavy griddle, turning once.

Yield: 12 pancakes

MAIN DISHES

getting to the core

PORK CHOPS ALA APPLES AND VEGETABLES

4   pork chops, about 3/4" thick
2   cooking apples
2   medium carrots
1/2   medium head cabbage, cut in wedges
1   cup apple juice
1   T. flour
1/2   tsp. salt
1/8   tsp. pepper

Brown pork chops slowly on both sides in heavy skillet. Place browned chops in baking dish. Peel and core apples. Slice in 1/2" thick slices and arrange on pork chops. To pan drippings, add flour and seasonings. Stir until browned. Add apple juice and cook until mixture boils and is slightly thickened. Add quartered carrots and cabbage wedges to meat. Pour thickened sauce over chops and vegetables. Cover.

Bake at 325° for 45 minutes. Serve pork chops and apple and vegetables with the sauce spooned over all.

Yield: 4 servings

A one-dish meal

PORK AND APPLE CHINESE DISH

1 1/2 # lean boneless pork
2 T. vegetable oil
1 tsp. ginger
1/4 tsp. garlic salt
1/2 small onion, sliced
1 tsp. Kitchen Bouquet
1 cup water
2 stalks celery, sliced
2 apples, peeled and sliced thin
1 (14 oz.) can bean sprouts
1 (8 oz.) can water chestnuts
1 (4 oz.) can mushrooms
Soy sauce to taste

2 T. cornstarch
1/3 cup cold water

Thinly slice pork. Place in heavy fry pan and brown in oil. Sprinkle ginger and garlic salt over meat. Sauté onions during last few minutes. Add water, Kitchen Bouquet, and cover; cook until pork is thoroughly cooked and very tender. Add celery, apples and soy sauce, cover, and continue simmering about 10 minutes.

Add drained bean sprouts and water chestnuts to meat mixture. Heat. Meanwhile, stir cornstarch into cold water and pour mixture over all. Add more soy sauce, if desired. Cook until heated through and the sauce is clear and transparent. Serve over cooked rice.

Yield: 6 servings

HAM 'N APPLES

1 ham slice, 3/4" thick
2 tart apples, peeled
1/8 tsp. cinnamon
1/8 tsp. nutmeg
1/4 cup brown sugar
1/2 cup water

Brown ham slightly on both sides in fry pan. Slash fat on ham to prevent curling. Place apple slices or rings over ham. Sprinkle with cinnamon, nutmeg, and brown sugar. Pour water in pan and cover. Cook approximately 30 minutes over low to medium heat, adding water, if necessary.

Yield: 4-6 servings

A winning combination

COMPANY STYLE MEAT LOAF

2# ground beef
1 1/2 cups seasoned stuffing mix
2 eggs
1 tsp. salt
2 cups cooking apples, peeled and finely chopped
1/2 small onion, minced
1/2 cup catsup
2 T. prepared horseradish
1 T. prepared mustard

Mix together all ingredients. Pack into well-greased 9" x 5" x 3" loaf pan. Bake at 350° for 60 minutes.

Yield: 8 servings

MEAT LOAF WITH ZESTY TOPPING

1 1/2 # ground beef
1/4 medium onion, minced
2 slices dry toast, cubed
3/4 cup applesauce
1 tsp. salt
1/4 tsp. pepper
2 T. catsup
2 T. brown sugar
1 tsp. dry mustard
1 tsp. prepared horseradish

Mix together thoroughly the ground beef, onions, dry bread cubes, applesauce and seasonings. Pack into 9" x 5" x 3" greased loaf pan. Combine catsup, brown sugar, mustard, and horseradish and spoon over top of loaf. Bake at 325° for 1 hour.

Yield: 6 servings

BEEF ROAST WITH CIDER

3#-4# beef roast, round or arm
1 medium onion, sliced
5 whole cloves
1 cinnamon stick
1/4 tsp. ginger
1 tsp. salt
2 cups apple cider

Marinate beef with onion, spices and cider 6 hours or overnight in refrigerator. Place meat and marinate in roasting pan and cover. Bake in 325° oven for 2 hours, or until tender. Serve with juices.

Yield: *6-8 servings*

A new twist to a favorite meal

SAUSAGES ALA FRUIT

1 large tart cooking apple
4 slices (rings) pineapple
3/4# pork sausage

Shape sausage into 4 patties. Fry sausage in frypan until thoroughly cooked. Keep sausages warm. Pour off excess grease.
Peel and core apples. Cut in 4 rings. Sauté apple rings and 4 rings of pineapple in 1 T. of the sausage fat. Serve sausages topped with apple and pineapple rings.

Yield: 4 servings

BAKED SQUASH WITH APPLES

2 acorn squash
2 cooking apples
1/4 cup cashew nuts
1/4 cup maple syrup
1/4 cup butter or margarine, melted
2 Smokie sausages

Cut squash in half crosswise. Take out seeds and stringy material. Dice peeled apples and slice sausages; fill squash centers. Over this, pour syrup, melted butter and nuts. Place squash in baking pan and cover with aluminum foil.

Bake at 350° for 45 minutes. Spoon drippings over squash and stuffing. If extra apples and sausages are left, place in small baking dish and bake with squash.

Yield: 4-8 servings

CAKES

pick of the crop

FRUITY APPLESAUCE CAKE WITH CARAMEL FROSTING

1 cup brown sugar
3/4 cup shortening
3 eggs
2 1/2 cups flour
3 tsp. baking powder
1 tsp. baking soda
1/2 tsp. salt
1 tsp. cinnamon
1/2 tsp. cloves
1 1/2 cups applesauce
1/2 cup raisins
1/2 cup nuts

Heat applesauce in saucepan on medium heat. Cream together brown sugar and shortening. Add eggs, beating well after each addition. Sift together dry ingredients, except baking soda, and add alternately with heated applesauce, to which the baking soda has been added. Mix well. Blend in raisins and nuts. Pour into greased and floured 9" x 13" pan. Bake at 375° for 35-40 minutes. Cool. Frost with caramel frosting:

1/2 cup butter or margarine
1 cup brown sugar
1/4 cup milk
2 cups sifted confectioners' sugar
1 tsp. vanilla

Melt butter in pan over low heat. Add brown sugar and cook for about 3 minutes. Add milk slowly and continue cooking until mixture comes to a full rolling boil, stirring constantly. Remove from heat and let cool. Then stir in confectioners' sugar, beating well after each addition. Add confectioners' sugar until frosting is of spreading consistency.

Yield: 16 servings

Note the procedure for heating applesauce and baking soda. Bubbly & light.

APPLE SPICE CAKE

1 3/4 cups sugar
1/2 cup shortening
3 eggs
1 1/2 cups applesauce
2 cups flour
1 tsp. baking soda
1/2 tsp. salt
1/2 tsp. cinnamon
1/4 tsp. cloves
1/2 cup raisins

Heat applesauce in saucepan over medium heat. Cream sugar and shortening in large mixing bowl. Beat in eggs, one at a time. Stir in flour, salt, and spices. Add baking soda to hot applesauce and blend into rest of mixture. Stir in raisins which have been plumped in 1 cup hot water and then drained well. Mix thoroughly. Pour into greased 9" x 13" cake pan.

Bake at 350° for 45-50 minutes. Cool. Serve with topping:

3 T. butter or margarine
1 egg
1/2 cup brown sugar
1/4 tsp. nutmeg
1 tsp. vanilla
1 cup whipped topping

In small saucepan, melt butter. Beat egg. Combine with brown sugar and add to butter. Cook over low heat until thickened, stirring constantly. Let cool.

Add vanilla and fold into whipped topping. Serve over cooled cake. Sprinkle crushed peanut brittle on top. (Can substitute 1/2 cup whipping cream, whipped, for the whipped topping.)

Yield: 16 servings

APPLE BUNDT CAKE

2 cups sugar
1 1/2 cups vegetable oil
3 eggs, beaten
2 tsp. vanilla
3 cups flour
1 tsp. baking soda
1 tsp. salt
3 cups grated raw apples
1 cup chopped nuts

In large mixing bowl, mix together sugar and oil. Add beaten eggs and vanilla. Stir in dry ingredients. Mixture will be thick. Fold in grated apples and nuts. Blend well. Pour into well-greased 10" Bundt pan.

Bake at 350° for 60-70 minutes. Let cool in pan for 15 minutes and then remove from pan to cool on rack. When cool, spread with the following topping:

Topping

1/2 cup butter or margarine
1/2 cup brown sugar
1/4 cup milk

Combine ingredients in small saucepan. Cook 3-4 minutes over medium heat, stirring constantly. Let cool without stirring, then beat until creamy with beater. Spread over top of cake and drizzle down sides. Garnish with additional nuts, if desired.

Yield: 20 servings

An absolute favorite!

APPLE-PINEAPPLE BUNDT CAKE

3 cups flour
1 tsp. baking powder
1 tsp. baking soda
1 tsp. salt
1 tsp. cinnamon
1 cup vegetable oil
1 1/4 cups sugar
1 tsp. vanilla
3 eggs
1 (8 oz.) can crushed pineapple, in heavy syrup, undrained
2 cups apples, peeled and grated
1/2 cup nuts

Sift together dry ingredients. In large mixing bowl, combine oil, sugar, and vanilla. Stir in half of dry ingredients, mixing thoroughly. Add eggs, one at a time. Beat well. Blend in crushed pineapple, grated apples, nuts, and remaining dry ingredients. Spoon into well-greased and floured 10" Bundt pan. Bake at 350° for 60-70 minutes, or until done.

Let cool in pan for 15 minutes, then turn out on rack. When cool, transfer to serving plate and sprinkle confectioners' sugar over top.

Yield: 20 servings

Moist, tender, good

APPLE SQUARES

1 cup sugar
1/2 cup shortening
1 egg
1/4 cup milk
1 cup flour
1 tsp. baking powder
1/2 tsp. salt
1/2 tsp. nutmeg
2 medium apples, peeled and chopped
1 tsp. vanilla

Cream together sugar and shortening. Add egg and milk. Stir in dry ingredients, apples, and vanilla. Spread into greased 9" x 9" pan.
Bake at 350° for 30-35 minutes.
Serve warm with following sauce:

Lemon Sauce

2 T. cornstarch
1/2 cup water
1/2 cup light corn syrup
2 T. butter or margarine
Juice and grated peel of 1 lemon

Mix together cornstarch and water in saucepan and add corn syrup. Cook over medium heat until mixture comes to a full boil. Boil for 5 minutes. Remove from heat. Add butter, lemon juice and lemon rind. Serve warm over cake.

Yield: 9-12 servings

The lemon sauce complements this apple cake

QUICK AND EASY SHEET CAKE

1 1/2 cups sugar
2 eggs
2 cups flour
1 tsp. baking soda
1 tsp. salt
1/2 tsp. cinnamon
1 1/2 cups applesauce
1/2 cup nuts

Mix together in order given. Pour into a well-greased 10" x 15" sheet cake pan, or jelly roll pan.

Bake at 350° for 20-25 minutes. Just before cake is finished baking, make the following topping:

Topping

3/4 cup sugar
1/2 cup (1 stick) butter or margarine
1 small can (1/2 cup) evaporated milk

Place mixture on heat and let boil for 5 minutes, stirring constantly. Add 1 cup coconut and spread immediately on the hot cake.

Yield: 24-30 squares

GLAZED DUTCH APPLE CAKE

1 1/2 cups sugar
2 cups apples, unpeeled, but diced
2 eggs, beaten
1/2 cup vegetable oil
2 cups flour
2 tsp. baking soda
1/2 tsp. salt
1 tsp. vanilla
1/2 cup nuts, chopped

2 cups apple juice

In mixing bowl, place diced apples and sugar. Let stand for 15 minutes. Then stir in eggs, oil, dry ingredients, and vanilla. Blend in nuts. Pour into greased and floured angel food cake pan or Bundt pan.

Bake at 350° for 50-60 minutes. Let cake cool in pan for 15 minutes, then invert on serving plate. Prick cake with toothpick and pour hot glaze over cake. Serve warm or cold.

Hot Glaze: Boil 2 cups apple juice over medium heat until reduced to 1 cup. Pour while hot over cake.

Yield: 24 servings

COCOA APPLESAUCE CAKE

1 1/2 cups sugar
1/2 cup (1 stick) butter or margarine
2 eggs
2 cups flour
2 tsp. baking soda
1/2 tsp. salt
3 T. cocoa
1 1/2 cups applesauce
6 oz. semi-sweetened chocolate chips

Cream together sugar and butter or margarine. Add eggs. Sift together the dry ingredients. Add to the creamed mixture alternately with the applesauce. Fold in chocolate chips. Pour in greased 9" x 13" pan.

Bake at 350° for 35-40 minutes. Cool. Frost with butter frosting:

Butter Frosting

1/4 cup (1/2 stick) butter or margarine, softened
1 tsp. vanilla
3 cups sifted confectioners' sugar
2-3 T. milk

Whip butter and vanilla until fluffy. Add confectioners' sugar with the milk, until of a good spreading consistency.

Yield: 16-20 servings

EARLY AMERICAN APPLE CAKE

2   cups sugar
1   cup shortening
2   eggs
2   tsp. vanilla
3   cups flour
2   tsp. baking powder
1   tsp. baking soda
1   tsp. salt
1   tsp. cinnamon
1/2   tsp. cloves
1/2   tsp. allspice
1   cup cold coffee
2   cups apples, peeled and diced

1/2   cup sugar
1   tsp. cinnamon
1/4   cup chopped nuts

Cream shortening and sugar. Add eggs and vanilla. Sift together dry ingredients and add to creamed mixture alternately with the coffee. Add apples. Pour into 9" x 13" greased pan.

Mix together sugar and cinnamon-nut mixture and sprinkle over top. Bake at 350° for 45 minutes. Serve warm.

Yield: 20 servings

MISSOURI UPSIDE DOWN CAKE

3 T. butter or margarine
3/4 cup brown sugar
1/4 tsp. cinnamon
2 cooking apples, peeled and sliced

1/3 cup shortening
1/3 cup sugar
2 eggs
1 tsp. vanilla
1 1/2 cups flour
2 tsp. baking powder
1/2 tsp. salt
2/3 cup milk

Melt butter in 9" round pan. Add brown sugar and stir until melted. Arrange sliced apples on sugar/butter mixture. Sprinkle cinnamon over apples.

Cream shortening and sugar. Blend in eggs and vanilla, beating thoroughly. Add dry ingredients alternately with milk. Pour over apples in pan.

Bake at 350° for 40-45 minutes, or until done. Turn out onto serving plate immediately. Serve with whipped cream or pistachio ice cream.

Yield: 6-8 servings

APPLE GINGERBREAD

2 T. (1/4 stick) butter or margarine
1/3 cup brown sugar
1 large cooking apple, peeled and cored
3 maraschino cherries
1/4 cup raisins

1/4 cup sugar
1/4 cup shortening
1 egg
1/3 cup molasses
1 1/2 cups flour
1 tsp. baking powder
1/2 tsp. baking soda
1/4 tsp. salt
1/4 tsp. ginger
1/2 cup sour milk

In 8" round cake pan, melt butter. Sprinkle brown sugar evenly over melted butter in pan. Arrange thick sliced apples over butter-brown sugar mixture. Fill center with halved maraschino cherries. Sprinkle raisins over all.

Cream shortening and sugar. Beat in egg and molasses. Stir in dry ingredients alternately with the sour milk. Pour batter over apple-brown sugar mixture.

Bake at 350° for 35-40 minutes, or until done. Turn onto serving plate immediately. Serve with lemon sauce:

Lemon Sauce

1/2 cup sugar
1/4 cup cornstarch
1 cup water
2 T. butter or margarine
2 T. lemon juice
1/2 tsp. grated lemon rind
Few drops yellow food coloring

Mix together sugar and cornstarch in small saucepan. Gradually stir in water and place over medium heat. Cook until mixture boils and thickens, stirring constantly.

Remove from heat and add butter, lemon juice, and rind. Add few drops yellow food coloring. Serve warm over gingerbread.

Yield: 6-8 servings

ROSY APPLE CAKE

1 cup flour
1 tsp. baking powder
1/4 tsp. salt
3 T. butter or margarine
1 egg beaten with 1 T. milk

4-5 medium cooking apples
1 (3 oz.) pkg. strawberry gelatin
1-2 T. sugar

Mix first three dry ingredients. Cut in butter. Add egg and milk mixture. Mix together thoroughly and press in bottom and up sides of an 8" round pan. Peel apples and slice into dough-lined pan. Sprinkle dry gelatin over top of apples. Add 1-2 T. sugar, depending on tartness of apples. Mix the following topping and sprinkle over apples:

Topping

3/4 cup sugar
3/4 cup flour
3/4 stick butter or margarine

Cut butter into sugar, flour mixture, until crumbly. Sprinkle over top of apples. Bake at 375° for 45 minutes.

Yield: 6-8 servings

A picture perfect special cake

APPLE SOUR CREAM CAKE

1/2 cup shortening
1 cup sugar
2 eggs
2 1/2 cups flour
2 tsp. baking powder
1 tsp. baking soda
1/2 tsp. salt
1/2 tsp. cinnamon
1/4 tsp. cloves
1/4 tsp. nutmeg
3/4 cup milk
1 tsp. vanilla
4 medium apples, peeled and chopped
1/2 cup nuts, chopped

1 cup (8 oz.) dairy sour cream
1/2 cup sugar
1/4 tsp. cinnamon
2 eggs, beaten

Cream shortening with the sugar. Add eggs and beat thoroughly. Add the dry ingredients alternately with milk. Blend in apples, vanilla, and nuts. Pour into a greased 9" x 13" baking pan.

Stir together the sour cream, 1/2 cup sugar, 1/2 tsp. cinnamon, and beaten eggs until well blended. Pour mixture over cake batter and spread evenly.

Bake at 350° for 40-45 minutes, or until done.

Yield: 16-20 servings

PAN APPLE CAKE

1 1/2 cups sugar
1/2 cup (1 stick) butter or margarine
2 eggs
1 tsp. vanilla
2 cups flour
2 tsp. baking soda
1 tsp. salt
1 tsp. cinnamon
1/2 tsp. cloves
2 cups apples, peeled and chopped
1/2 cup pecans

Cream sugar and butter. Add eggs and vanilla. Mix in dry ingredients. Batter will be thick. Stir in chopped apples and pecans. Spread in greased and floured 9" x 13" pan.

Bake at 325° for 40-45 minutes. While warm, spread with following glaze:

Glaze

1 cup brown sugar
1/4 cup half and half cream
3 T. butter or margarine

Combine ingredients in saucepan over medium heat and bring to full boil, stirring constantly. Let boil 1 minute, then remove from heat. Cool slightly. Spread on warm cake.

Yield: 16-20 servings

AUTUMN APPLE CAKE

2 cups sugar
3/4 cup vegetable oil
2 eggs
1 tsp. vanilla
4 cups apples, peeled and grated
2 cups flour
2 tsp. baking powder
1 tsp. salt
1 tsp. cinnamon
1/2 cup walnuts

Mix together sugar, oil, eggs, and vanilla. Blend in apples. Sift together dry ingredients and add to mixture. Fold in nuts. Spread in greased 9" x 13" pan.

Bake at 350° for 45 minutes. Cool. Frost with cream cheese frosting:

Cream Cheese Frosting

1/4 cup (1/2 stick) butter or margarine, softened
1 (3 oz.) pkg. cream cheese
2 cups confectioners' sugar, sifted
1 tsp. vanilla

Cream together softened butter or margarine and cream cheese. Add vanilla. Slowly stir in confectioners' sugar until of spreading consistency. Frost.

Yield: 16-20 servings

HONEY TOPPED APPLE CAKE

3/4 cup sugar
1/2 cup shortening
2 eggs
2 cups flour
1 1/2 tsp. baking powder
1/4 tsp. salt
3/4 cup milk
1 tsp. vanilla
2 cups apples, peeled and sliced

3 T. sugar
1/4 tsp. cinnamon

Cream sugar and shortening. Add eggs. Sift dry ingredients and add to creamed mixture alternately with the milk.

Spread in greased 8" x 11" baking pan. Arrange apple slices over batter.

Combine sugar and cinnamon and sprinkle over top. Bake at 350° for 40-45 minutes. Serve warm with following sauce:

Sauce

1/4 cup sugar
1/2 cup brown sugar
1/4 cup (1/2 stick) butter or margarine
1/4 cup honey
1/2 cup milk

Combine all ingredients in small saucepan and place over medium heat, stirring to prevent sticking. Bring just to a boil. Serve hot over warm cake.

Yield: 8-10 servings

MOIST AND NUTTY APPLE CAKE

1 1/2 cups brown sugar
1/2 cup shortening
2 eggs
2 tsp. vanilla
1 cup sour milk or buttermilk
2 cups flour
2 tsp. baking soda
1 tsp. nutmeg
1/2 tsp. salt
2 cups apples, peeled and diced
1 cup chopped walnuts

Cream shortening and sugar. Add eggs and vanilla. Stir in dry ingredients alternately with sour milk or buttermilk. Fold in diced apples and walnuts.

Pour into greased 9" x 13" pan. Bake at 350° for 35-40 minutes. When cool, sprinkle with confectioners' sugar.

Yield: 16-20 servings

TOPPING FOR APPLE CAKES

3/4 cup brown sugar
3 T. milk
2 tsp. light corn syrup
1 T. butter or margarine
1/4 cup nuts, chopped

In saucepan, combine brown sugar, milk, corn syrup, and butter. Cook over medium heat, slowly bringing to a boil. Remove from heat. Serve over baked cake. Sprinkle with nuts.

1/2 cup brown sugar
1 T. cornstarch
1 cup water
3 T. butter or margarine
1 tsp. vanilla

In saucepan, blend cornstarch with brown sugar. Add water. Cook over medium heat until thick and clear. Remove from heat; add butter and vanilla. Serve over baked cake.

6 T. brown sugar
3 T. milk
3 T. butter or margarine
1 cup confectioners' sugar
1 tsp. vanilla

In small saucepan, combine brown sugar, milk, and butter or margarine. Slowly bring to a boil. Remove from heat. Add vanilla and enough confectioners' sugar until of drizzling consistency.

PIES and PASTRIES

tempting & appeeling

DUTCH APPLE PIE

1 1/4 cups flour
1 tsp. sugar
1 tsp. baking powder
1/2 tsp. salt
1/2 cup (1 stick) butter or margarine
1 egg yolk
2 T. milk

4 large apples, peeled and sliced
1/2 cup sugar
1 T. flour
1/4 tsp. cinnamon
1 T. butter or margarine

Measure dry ingredients into bowl. Cut in butter or margarine. Mix egg yolk with 2 T. milk and add to crumb mixture. Mix well and form dough into a ball. Pat with fingers into a 9" pie pan.

Place sliced apples in dough lined pan. Sprinkle the mixture of sugar, flour, and cinnamon over top. Dot with butter.

Bake in 375° oven for 45 minutes.

CHEESY APPLE PIE

1 unbaked 9" pie crust

6 tart cooking apples, peeled and thinly sliced
3/4 cup sugar
2 T. flour
3/4 tsp. cinnamon
1/8 tsp. cloves
1/8 tsp. salt
1 tsp. grated lemon peel

Combine sugar, flour, spices, salt, and lemon peel. Add apples and lightly toss to mix. Arrange apples in unbaked 9" pie crust. Sprinkle cheese-crumb topping over apples:

Cheese-Crumb Topping

1/4 cup sugar
1/2 cup flour
1/2 cup grated cheddar cheese
1/4 cup (1/2 stick) butter or margarine, melted

Mix together sugar, flour, and cheese with the melted butter. Sprinkle mixture over apples.
    Bake in 400° oven for 40 minutes, or until lightly browned.

APPLE MINCEMEAT PIE

1   9" unbaked pie shell

2   cups prepared mincemeat
4   medium apples, peeled and sliced
Juice of 1/2 lemon
1/3   cup sugar
1/2   cup flour
1/2   cup brown sugar
1/4   cup (1/2 stick) butter or margarine

In unbaked pie shell, spread prepared mincemeat. Mix apples lightly with lemon juice and sugar and spread over mincemeat.

Mix together flour and brown sugar. Cut in butter and sprinkle crumb mixture over apples.

Bake in 425° oven for 15 minutes, then lower oven temperature to 325° and continue baking 45 minutes, or until lightly browned.

CARAMEL APPLE PIE

1 cup brown sugar
3 T. flour
1/4 tsp. salt
3/4 cup water
1 T. lemon juice
1 tsp. vanilla
1 T. butter
4 large apples, peeled and sliced

Pastry for 9" pie crust
2 T. brown sugar

In saucepan, mix together brown sugar, flour, and salt. Stir in water and lemon juice. Cook until thickened. Remove from heat and add vanilla and butter. Let cool.

Place apples in pastry-lined pan. Pour cooked mixture over apples in pie pan. Crumble the excess pastry with the 2 T. brown sugar and sprinkle crumbs on top.

Bake in 425° oven for 15 minutes, then reduce oven temperature to 375° and continue baking for 30-35 minutes.

Very good flavor

APPLE SOUR CREAM PIE

Pastry for 9" one-crust pie

3/4 cup sugar
2 T. flour
1/4 tsp. salt
1/4 tsp. cinnamon
1/4 tsp. nutmeg
1 egg, unbeaten
1 cup dairy sour cream
1 tsp. vanilla
4 medium apples, peeled and sliced

Roll out pastry for single crust 9" pie. In bowl, stir together sugar, flour, salt and spices. Add egg, vanilla, and sour cream. Beat smooth. Blend in apples and turn into pastry-lined pie plate.

Bake at 400° for 15 minutes, then reduce oven temperature to 350° and bake for 30 minutes. Remove from oven and sprinkle with streusel topping:

Streusel Topping

3 T. sugar
3 T. flour
3 T. butter or margarine
1/4 cup nuts, chopped
1/2 tsp. cinnamon

Combine ingredients and mix until crumbly. Sprinkle over pie and return to oven. Bake for 10 additional minutes, or until lightly browned.

OLD FAVORITE APPLE PIE

Pastry for 2 crust 9" pie:
2 cups flour
1 tsp. salt
3/4 cup shortening
5—7 T. cold water

Mix flour and salt in medium mixing bowl. Cut in shortening with pastry blender or 2 knives until particles are the size of peas.

Sprinkle water over the mixture, 1 T. at a time, using a fork to toss, until all flour is moistened. Gather into a ball. Refrigerate for 1/2-1 hour.

Roll out 1/2 of dough at a time. Lightly flour a board and rolling pin. Turn 1/2 of dough into a ball and flatten. Roll lightly from center out until dough is about 1/8" thick and fits a 9" pie pan. Fold in fourths and transfer to pan, being careful not to stretch dough. Trim, allowing a 1" overhang. Roll second half of dough for top crust. Prepare filling.

6 cups tart apples, peeled and sliced

3/4 cup sugar
1/2 tsp. cinnamon
1 T. butter

1 T. sugar

Mix sugar and cinnamon lightly through apples. Pile into pastry lined pan. Dot with butter. Cover with top crust; make decorative slashes in top crust to allow steam to escape. Seal ends and flute edge. Sprinkle 1 T. sugar over top of pie.

Bake in 425° oven for 15 minutes, then reduce heat to 375° and continue baking for 35-40 minutes, or until crust is lightly browned.

What can one say about an old favorite ??

ONE-CRUST HONEY APPLE PIE

1 unbaked 9" pie crust

5 cups apples, peeled and sliced
3 T. cornstarch
2 T. butter or margarine, melted
1/4 cup honey
1 T. lemon juice

In mixing bowl, stir together the cornstarch and melted butter. Add honey and lemon juice. Mix in apple slices and toss to coat. Pour into pastry-lined pan.

Sprinkle nut topping over apples.

Nut Topping

1/3 cup brown sugar
3/4 cup flour
1/4 tsp. nutmeg
1/3 cup butter
1/4 cup nuts, chopped

Combine brown sugar, flour, and nutmeg. Cut in butter until crumbly. Add nuts.

Bake at 400° for 15 minutes, then reduce heat and bake at 350° for 30-40 minutes, or until topping and crust are lightly brown.

Mild, honey flavor

APPLE STREUSEL TOPPED PIE

1   9" unbaked pie crust

6   medium apples, peeled and sliced
3/4   cup sugar
1/2   tsp. cinnamon
1   T. flour

Mix together lightly the apples, sugar, flour, and cinnamon. Turn into unbaked pie crust. In small bowl, combine the following for streusel topping.

Streusel Topping

1/4   cup granulated sugar
1/4   cup brown sugar
1/2   cup butter or margarine
3/4   cup flour
1/4   tsp. cinnamon

Combine all ingredients until crumbly and sprinkle over apples.
Bake at 425° for 15 minutes. Reduce oven temperature to 350° and continue baking 30-35 minutes.

APPLE MERINGUE PIE

1/3 cup butter or margarine
3 T. sugar
2 egg yolks
3/4 cup flour
Rind of 1/2 lemon

5 medium cooking apples
1/3 cup sugar
Juice of 1/2 lemon

1/2 cup raspberry jam

2 egg whites
1/4 cup sugar
1 tsp. vanilla

Cream together butter and 3 T. sugar until light and fluffy. Add egg yolks and beat well. Add flour and grated rind of 1/2 lemon. Mix until well blended. Press into bottom of greased 9" pie pan.

Bake in 350° oven for 15-20 minutes.

In saucepan, combine apples which have been peeled and sliced, 1/3 cup sugar, and juice of 1/2 lemon. Cook until tender. Cool.

Spread jam on bottom of cooled crust in pie pan. Layer cooked apples on top. Beat the 2 egg whites with 1/4 cup sugar, beating in 1 T. at a time, until sugar is dissolved and stiff peaks form. Beat in vanilla. Pile meringue on apples.

Bake in 350° oven for 15 minutes, or until lightly browned.

APPLE PECAN PIE

1/4 cup (1/2 stick) butter or margarine, softened
1/4 cup pecan halves
1/2 cup brown sugar

Pastry for 2 crust pie

5 cups apples, peeled and sliced
1 T. lemon juice
2 T. flour
2/3 cup sugar
1/2 tsp. cinnamon
1/4 tsp. nutmeg

In 9" pie pan, spread softened butter on bottom of pan. Press pecan halves, flat side up, into butter and pat brown sugar over all.

Roll out pastry for 1 crust and place in pan over mixture, leaving 1/2" overhang. Trim. In pie crust place the sliced apples which have been mixed with rest of ingredients.

Roll out top crust, place on apples, trim and flute edges. Make slashes in top crust. Place pan or foil under pie to catch juices.

Bake at 425° for 10 minutes, and then reduce heat to 350° and continue baking 45 minutes more.

Remove from oven and let set until bubbling stops. Then place serving plate over pie and invert, being careful with the hot syrup mixture. Good served warm or cold.

DEEP DISH APPLE PIE

Pastry:

2 cups flour
3/4 cup sugar
1 1/2 tsp. baking powder
1/2 cup (1 stick) butter or margarine
2 egg yolks

Filling:

6 medium apples
1/2 cup sugar
1/4 cup water
1 T. lemon juice

For pastry, mix together dry ingredients. Cut in butter until mixture is crumbly. Add egg yolks and blend well. Reserve 1 cup of crumbs for topping and pat remainder in bottom and up sides of 10" pie pan.

For filling, peel and slice apples. Add sugar, water and lemon juice. Cook over medium heat until apples are tender. Cool.

Fill pastry-lined pie pan with cooled apples. Sprinkle remainder of crumbs on top.

Bake in 325° oven for 40-45 minutes.

*Makes a good sized pie
with an easy-to-make crust*

UPSIDE DOWN PIE

Pastry for 1 9" pie crust

4 cups apples, peeled and sliced
1/4 cup sugar
2 T. brown sugar
1/2 tsp. cinnamon
1 tsp. butter

Place peeled and sliced apples in ungreased 9" pie pan. Sprinkle 1/4 cup sugar over top of apples.

Roll out pastry for single pie crust and place pie crust over apples, pressing down and fluting edge. Prick crust with fork.

Bake at 375° for 35-45 minutes, or until crust is slightly brown and apples are tender. Let cool for 15 minutes, then invert on serving plate. Sprinkle with the brown sugar, cinnamon and butter. Serve warm with ice cream.

BOTTOMLESS PIE

4-6 apples, peeled and sliced
1 cup brown sugar
1 cup flour
1/4 tsp. nutmeg
1/2 tsp. cinnamon
1/2 cup (1 stick) butter or margarine, softened
1 egg

Place sliced apples in greased 9" pie pan. Mix together softened butter, brown sugar, flour, spices and egg. Drop by teaspoons on top of apples.

Bake at 350° for 35-45 minutes.

*An old German custom dictates
pouring cream over serving before eating.*

OLD FASHIONED APPLE STRUDEL

Dough

    2 cups flour
    1/4 tsp. salt
    1 egg, beaten
    1 T. vegetable oil
    1/2 cup lukewarm water

Measure flour and salt into bowl. Make well in flour and stir in beaten egg, oil, and water. Mix well until a soft dough forms. Knead dough until smooth and elastic, about 10 minutes. Cover air tight (in plastic bag). Let rest in warm place for 1 hour or more.

Filling

    8-10 medium apples, peeled and thinly sliced
    1 1/2 cups sugar
    1/2 tsp. cinnamon
    1/2 cup crushed corn flakes
    1/2 cup (1 stick) butter or margarine

Peel and slice apples. Mix with the sugar, crumbs, and cinnamon just before spreading on the dough. Melt butter; let cool.

Roll out dough on table on a well-floured tablecloth. Roll, then pull and stretch dough until paper thin. Pour melted butter over dough and spread apples over 2/3 of dough. Begin rolling on end with apple mixture. Roll into tight loaf. Stretch and pull as you roll. Seal all edges and fold under at ends. Place in U shape on greased cookie sheet which has sides to catch juices. Score the top in several places.

Bake at 350° for 1 hour to 1 1/2 hour, turning oven down to 325° last 20 minutes, until nicely browned. Baste with melted butter several times while baking. Sprinkle sugar generously on roll about 5 minutes before it is done baking.

Yield: 10-12 servings

Makes a tender delicious, unbeatable strudel!

PATTI'S FRESH FRUIT PIZZA

1   pkg. refrigerator sugar cookie dough
8   oz. cream cheese, softened
1/3   cup sugar
2   T. milk
1   T. orange rind
1   tsp. vanilla
3   red Delicious apples
2   bananas
1   cup pineapple chunks, drained
10   fresh strawberries, sliced
Glaze
1/2   cup sugar
1   T. cornstarch
1/4   tsp. salt
1/2   cup orange juice   *Looks & tastes ever so good!*
1/4   cup water
1   T. lemon juice
1   T. lemon rind

Divide cookie dough in half. Place 1/2 softened cookie dough in each of two 9" greased pie pans. Spread with fingers up sides of buttered pans. Prick bottom and sides with fork. Bake 10-12 minutes at 350°. Cool.

Mix softened cream cheese with sugar, milk, and orange rind. Spread this over the cooled crusts.

Core and slice unpeeled apples, which have been dipped in pineapple juice, and arrange over cream cheese mixture. Slice bananas and strawberries and arrange. Place pineapple chunks over the pizza top.

To make the glaze, in saucepan mix together sugar, cornstarch, and salt. Gradually pour in juice and water. Add lemon rind. Bring mixture to a boil and cook 1 minute. Cool.

Drizzle glaze over fruit and chill. Cut into wedge size pieces.

Yield: 12-15 servings.

APPLE PASTRY FOR A CROWD

Rich Pastry

5 cups flour
1 T. sugar
1/2 tsp. salt
1/2 tsp. baking powder
1 1/2 cups shortening
2 egg yolks
Cold water

Measure dry ingredients into large mixing bowl. Cut in shortening until particles are size of peas. Place egg yolks in measuring cup and stir with fork. Add water to measure 1 cup. Gradually sprinkle over dry ingredients, tossing with a fork to moisten. Gather into a ball and refrigerate for 30 minutes. Then divide dough in half and line an ungreased 10 1/2" x 15 1/2" jelly roll pan with the pastry. Add apple filling.

14-16 medium apples, peeled and sliced
2 T. lemon juice
1 cup brown sugar
1 cup granulated sugar
1 tsp. cinnamon
1/2 tsp. nutmeg
1/4 tsp. cloves
2 T. butter or margarine

Sprinkle lemon juice over apples. Combine sugars and spices. Arrange half of the apples evenly on bottom of pastry-lined pan. Sprinkle half of the sugar-spice mixture over apples. Add remaining apples on top and sprinkle with rest of sugar-spice mixture. Dot with butter. Roll out top crust; seal and flute edges. Cut vents in top crust to allow steam to escape.

Bake in 400 ° oven for 45-55 minutes. When cool, drizzle vanilla glaze over top.

Vanilla Glaze

1 cup confectioners' sugar
1 T. soft butter or margarine
2-3 T. milk
1/2 tsp. vanilla

Combine all ingredients until of correct consistency to pour over pastry. Cut into squares.

Yield: 24 servings

*Rather than making four pies for 24 people,
make one large pastry for 24*

COMPANY APPLE SQUARES

2 cups flour
1/2 tsp. salt
2/3 cup shortening
2 egg yolks
1/3 to 1/2 cup cold water

In mixing bowl, combine flour and salt. Cut in shortening. Blend egg yolks with water and mix into mixture until a soft dough forms and holds together. Divide dough in half. Roll out 1/2 and line bottom and sides of 9" x 13" pan with pastry. Fill with apple filling:

4-5 cups apples, peeled and sliced
3/4-1 cup sugar
1 T. flour
1/2 tsp. cinnamon
1/4 tsp. nutmeg
1 T. butter

Toss apples lightly with dry ingredients. Spread in pastry lined pan. Dot with butter.

Roll out second half of dough and cover apples. Pinch edges of dough and flute. Cut slits in top crust.

Bake at 400° for 40-50 minutes, or until lightly brown. When done but still warm, drizzle following icing over top:

1 cup confectioners' sugar
2 T. butter or margarine, softened
1 1/2 oz. cream cheese, softened
1 tsp. vanilla
1 tsp. milk

Mix together softened butter and cream cheese. Gradually mix in confectioners' sugar, milk, and vanilla, until of a consistency to drizzle over top.

Do you need to make a large dessert?

Yield: 24 servings

Try this frosted apple-filled pastry

APPLE PASTRY FOLD-OVERS

1 1/2 cups flour
1/2 tsp. salt
1/2 cup (1 stick) butter or margarine
4-6 T. cold water

2 medium apples, peeled and sliced
1/4 cup sugar
1 T. flour
1/4 tsp. cinnamon
2 T. walnuts, chopped
1 T. butter or margarine

Mix together flour and salt. Cut in butter. Sprinkle crumbed mixture with water, a tablespoon at a time. Stirring with fork, add just enough water to moisten. Gather dough into a ball and refrigerate for 30 minutes. Then roll out on lightly-floured board to fit size of cookie sheet. Place on ungreased cookie sheet. Mix apples lightly with the sugar, flour, cinnamon mixture. Arrange apples down the center third of pastry. Fold sides to middle and about 1" at each end. Sprinkle walnuts down center. Dot with butter. Brush pastry with cream before baking.

Bake at 425° for 20-30 minutes, or until lightly brown. Drizzle vanilla icing over top.

Vanilla Icing

1 cup confectioners' sugar
1-2 T. milk
1/2 tsp. vanilla

Combine ingredients. Add enough milk to form a thin icing.

Or, melt 1/4 cup apricot jam. Add approximately 2 T. cognac and pour over apples. Serve warm or cold.

Yield: 10 servings

The jam-cognac mixture adds an interesting flavor.

OLD WORLD APPLE CREAM PIE

1   9"   unbaked pie crust

4   cups apples, peeled and sliced
3/4   cup sugar
2   T. flour
1/2   tsp. nutmeg
3/4   cup cream
1   tsp. vanilla
1/4   tsp. cinnamon
1   T. butter or margarine

Peel and slice apples into unbaked pie crust. Combine sugar, flour, and nutmeg, and spoon over apples. Sprinkle with cinnamon and dot with butter. Pour cream and vanilla mixture over all.

Bake in 375° oven for 50-60 minutes, or until apples are tender and crust is lightly brown.

COUNTRY APPLE CUSTARD PIE

Pastry for 9" pie crust and strips for top

1 cup thick apple butter or applesauce
3 eggs, beaten
1/2 cup sugar
1/4 cup (1/2 stick) butter or margarine, melted
1/2 tsp. nutmeg

Into 3 beaten eggs, add sugar and melted butter. Blend in apple butter or sauce. Pour into unbaked 9" pie crust. Sprinkle top with nutmeg. Lattice top with pastry strips.

Bake in 350° oven for 40-45 minutes. When cool, sprinkle confectioners' sugar over pie and serve.

CUSTARD APPLE PIE

1/2 cup apple butter
2 eggs, beaten
1/2 cup sugar
2 T. cornstarch
1/2 tsp. cinnamon
1/4 tsp. nutmeg
1 3/4 cups milk

Pastry for 9" pie

Thoroughly combine apple butter, beaten eggs, sugar, cornstarch, and spices. Gradually stir in milk and blend well. Pour filling into unbaked pastry shell.

Bake in 375° oven for 50-60 minutes.

APPLE DUMPLINGS

Pastry Crust

2   cups flour
2   tsp. baking powder
1/4 tsp. salt
1/2 cup shortening
4-6 T. milk

Apples

6   apples, peeled and cored
1/4 cup sugar
1/2 tsp. cinnamon
2   T. butter or margarine

Sauce

1 1/2 cups sugar
2   cups water
1/4 tsp. cinnamon
1   T. butter or margarine
1/4 cup orange juice

Roll out pastry crust and cut into six squares. Place peeled and cored apple in center of square. Fill cavity of each apple with mixture of cinnamon and sugar. Dot with butter. Bring 4 corners up and over apple to encase each in pastry. Place in 9" x 13" baking pan.

Boil ingredients for sauce until sugar is dissolved. Pour this sauce *around* apple dumplings

Bake in 375° oven for 40-45 minutes, until lightly brown and apples are tender.

Yield: 6 servings

What a great fall treat!

APPLE ROLL

Dough

1 1/2 cups flour
2 tsp. baking powder
1/2 tsp. salt
1/4 cup shortening
4-6 T. milk

Apple Filling

4 medium apples, peeled and sliced
2 T. butter or margarine

Sauce

1 cup sugar
1 cup hot water
1/2 tsp. cinnamon
2 T. butter or margarine

Blend together flour, baking powder, and salt. Cut in shortening. Add enough milk to make a soft dough. Roll out dough into rectangular shape. Place sliced apples over dough and dot with butter. Starting at wide end, roll up in one long roll. Slice roll in 1 1/2" slices and place cut side down in greased 8" x 11" pan.

To make sauce, boil together sugar, water, and cinnamon for 3 minutes. Add butter. Pour hot sauce over and around slices.

Bake in 350° oven for 35-45 minutes, or until lightly browned.

Yield: 8-10 servings

Dish out while still warm

COOKIES

sweet blossoms

APPLE COOKIES

2 1/4 cups flour
1 tsp. baking powder
1 tsp. baking soda
1/2 tsp. salt
1/4 tsp. cinnamon
1/4 tsp. nutmeg
1/2 cup (1 stick) butter or margarine
1 cup brown sugar
1 egg
1/4 cup milk
2 cups apples, peeled and grated
1/2 cup chopped nuts

Sift dry ingredients. Cream butter and brown sugar. Add egg. Stir in dry ingredients with milk, apples, and nuts. Mix well. Drop by teaspoon on greased cookie sheet.

Bake at 375° for 10-12 minutes. Glaze with following while still warm:

Glaze

1 cup confectioners' sugar
1 T. soft butter or margarine
1—2 T. milk
1/2 tsp. vanilla

Yield: 3-4 dozen

Very moist & tender

REFRIGERATOR APPLE NUT COOKIES

1 cup granulated sugar
1 cup brown sugar
1 cup shortening
2 eggs
2 tsp. vanilla
3 1/2 cups flour
1 tsp. baking powder
1 tsp. baking soda
1/2 tsp. salt
1/2 tsp. nutmeg
1 cup applesauce
1 cup coconut
1/2 cup nuts, chopped

Cream together the sugars and shortening. Add eggs and vanilla. Stir in dry ingredients. Blend in applesauce, coconut, and nuts. Refrigerate at least 2 hours or overnight. Drop by teaspoonfuls on well-greased cookie sheet.

Bake at 350° for 12-15 minutes.

Yield: 4-5 dozen

EASY MOIST APPLE DROPS

1   cup sugar
1   cup shortening
1   egg
1   cup thick applesauce
1   tsp. vanilla
2   cups flour
1   tsp. baking powder
1   tsp. baking soda
1/2   tsp. salt
1/2   tsp. cinnamon
1/2   cup nuts, chopped

Cream sugar and shortening. Add egg, applesauce, and vanilla. Stir in dry ingredients and nuts. Drop by teaspoon on greased cookie sheet.
Bake at 350° for 12-15 minutes.

Yield: 3 dozen

SPICY APPLESAUCE COOKIES

2 1/4　cups flour
1　tsp. baking powder
1/2　tsp. salt
1/2　tsp. cinnamon
1/4　tsp. nutmeg
1/8　tsp. cloves
1/2　cup shortening
1　cup sugar, brown or white
1　egg
1　cup applesauce
1/2　cup raisins

Combine applesauce and raisins and set aside. Sift dry ingredients. In mixing bowl, cream shortening and sugar. Add egg and beat well. Mix in applesauce and raisins, and dry ingredients. Drop with teaspoon on lightly greased cookie sheet.
Bake at 350° for 12-15 minutes.

Yield:　4 dozen

APPLE MOLASSES COOKIES

2 1/2 cups flour
1 tsp. baking soda
1/2 tsp. salt
1/2 tsp. cinnamon
1/4 tsp. ginger
1/4 tsp. cloves
1/4 tsp. allspice
1/2 cup (1 stick) butter or margarine
1/2 cup brown sugar
1/2 cup granulated sugar
1 egg
1/4 cup molasses
1 cup peeled and grated apples
1/2 cup nuts, chopped

Cream butter and sugars. Add egg and molasses. Stir in dry ingredients. Blend in apples and nuts. Drop by teaspoon onto lightly greased cookie sheet.
Bake at 375° for 10-12 minutes.

Yield: 3-4 dozen

Moist-with a mellow molasses flavor

APPLES 'N HONEY COOKIES

1/2 cup shortening
3/4 cup honey
1 egg
1 tsp. vanilla
2 medium apples, grated
2 1/2 cups flour
1 tsp. baking soda
1/2 tsp. salt
1/2 tsp. cinnamon
1/2 tsp. cloves
1/2 cup walnuts, chopped

Blend together shortening and honey. Add egg and vanilla.
Stir in apples. Sift together dry ingredients and add to mixture.
Fold in nuts. Drop dough by teaspoon on greased cookie sheet.
Bake at 350° for 8-10 minutes.

Yield: 3-4 dozen

DROP OATMEAL APPLE COOKIES

1/2 cup (1 stick) butter or margarine
3/4 cup sugar
1 egg
2 cups flour
1 tsp. baking powder
1/2 tsp. salt
1/2 tsp. cinnamon
1/4 tsp. cloves
1 1/2 cups quick rolled oats
1 cup applesauce
1/4 cup nuts, chopped

Cream butter and sugar. Add egg. Sift dry ingredients and add to creamed mixture. Stir in oatmeal, apples and nuts. Drop with teaspoon on lightly greased cookie sheet.
Bake at 375° for 15-18 minutes.

Yield: 3 dozen

Packed with good nutrition –
apples, oatmeal & nuts

FROSTED APPLESAUCE BARS

1/2 cup butter or margarine
2/3 cup brown sugar
1 egg
1 cup flour
1 tsp. baking soda
1/2 tsp. salt
1/2 tsp. cinnamon
1/4 tsp. nutmeg
1 cup applesauce
1/2 cup nuts

Cream butter and brown sugar. Add egg. Stir in sifted dry ingredients, except baking soda. Heat applesauce in pan. Add baking soda to applesauce and quickly stir into batter. Blend in nuts. Spread in well greased 9" x 9" pan.

Bake at 350° for 30-35 minutes, or until toothpick inserted in center comes out clean. When cool, spread with the following frosting:

Frosting

1/2 cup brown sugar
2 T. milk
1 T. butter or margarine
2 cups confectioners' sugar

In small pan, place brown sugar, milk and butter and bring to a boil. Cook 2 minutes at medium heat, stirring constantly. When cool, add confectioners' sugar until of spreading consistency.

Yield: 8-10 bars

SOUR CREAM APPLE BARS

2   cups flour
1 1/2   cups brown sugar
1/2   cup (1   stick) butter or margarine, softened
1/4   cup chopped nuts

1   tsp. baking soda
1/2   tsp. salt
1   tsp. cinnamon
1   cup sour cream
1   egg, beaten
1   tsp. vanilla
2   cups apples, peeled and grated

In mixing bowl, combine flour, brown sugar and butter until crumbly. Add nuts. Press 1/2 of this mixture into ungreased 9" x 13" pan. To remainder of crumbly mixture, add baking soda, salt, cinnamon, sour cream, egg, and vanilla. Mix well. Stir in grated apples. Spoon over crumbs in pan.

Bake at 350° for 25-30 minutes.

Yield: 20 bars

A 'teachers' lounge' special!

MOLASSES BARS

1   cup shortening
1/2   cup brown sugar
1   cup granulated sugar
2   eggs
1/2   cup molasses
1/2   cup sour cream
2 1/2   cups flour
2   tsp. baking powder
1/2   tsp. baking soda
1/2   tsp. salt
1/2   tsp. cinnamon
1/4   tsp. cloves
2   medium apples, peeled and chopped
1/4   cup nuts, chopped

Cream shortening and sugars. Add eggs, molasses, and sour cream. Mix well. Blend in apples. Stir in dry ingredients and nuts. Spread in greased 15 1/2" x 10 1/2" baking pan.

Bake at 350° for 15 minutes, then decrease oven temperature to 325° and bake for 15-20 additional minutes. Cool. Dust with confectioners' sugar. Cut into bars.

Yield: 3 dozen bars

CHUNKY APPLE BARS

1 1/2 cups flour
1 tsp. baking powder
1/2 tsp. salt
1 egg
1/2 cup sugar
1/3 cup vegetable oil
1/2 tsp. cinnamon
1 tsp. vanilla
1/4 cup nuts
1 (20 oz.) can prepared apple pie filling
1/2 cup graham cracker crumbs
1/4 cup brown sugar
2 T. butter or margarine, melted
1/4 tsp. nutmeg

Cream flour, baking powder and salt. In mixing bowl, beat egg, add sugar, oil, cinnamon, vanilla, and nuts. Stir in flour mixture. Blend well. Spread dough in well greased 15 1/2" x 10 1/2" x 1" baking sheet, almost to edges.

Bake in 375° oven for 10-12 minutes.

Spread prepared apple pie filling over cooled baked layer, to edge of crust. Mix together graham cracker crumbs, brown sugar, melted butter and nutmeg. Sprinkle over apple mixture.

Broil 6" from heat until lightly browned and bubbly.

Yield: 24 squares

Very good-and easy to make

FAST APPLE SQUARES

1/4 cup (1/2 stick) butter or margarine
3/4 cup sugar
1 egg, beaten
1 tsp. vanilla
1 cup flour
1 tsp. baking powder
1/4 tsp. salt
1/4 tsp. cinnamon
1/4 tsp. nutmeg
1 medium cooking apple, peeled and chopped
1/4 cup nuts, chopped

In medium saucepan, melt butter. Remove from heat and add sugar. Cool slightly and add beaten egg and vanilla. Beat well. Stir in dry ingredients. Blend in apple and chopped nuts. Spread in well-greased 9" x 9" square pan.

Bake in 350° oven for 30-35 minutes. Cut into squares while warm. Dust confectioners' sugar over top when cool.

Yield: 16 squares

All mixed in one pan

DESSERTS

sweetened by nature

FAVORITE APPLE BETTY

4   cups cooking apples, peeled and sliced
1/3   cup sugar
1   tsp. cinnamon
3/4   cup hot water

Combine apples, sugar, cinnamon, and water. Simmer 10 minutes or until tender. Pour into ungreased 9" pie pan. Sprinkle the following crumb topping over the apples:

Topping

1/2   cup brown sugar
1/4   cup shortening
2   T. butter or margarine
1   cup flour
1   tsp. baking powder
1/4   tsp. salt

Blend brown sugar, shortening and butter. Add remaining ingredients and mix well. Mixture will be crumbly. Sprinkle over apples.
Bake at 350° for 25-30 minutes. Serve warm or cold.

Yield: 6 servings

*Call it Apple Betty, Brown Betty or Blue Betty,
it is absolutely the best Betty!*

APPLE BROWN BETTY

4-5 apples, peeled and sliced
1/3 cup sugar
1/2 tsp. cinnamon

1 cup flour
3/4 cup brown sugar
6 T. (3/4 stick) butter or margarine

Peel and slice apples. Place in lightly greased 9" x 9" pan. Sprinkle sugar and cinnamon over apples.

Mix together flour and brown sugar. Cut in butter. Mixture will be crumbly. Sprinkle over apples in pan.

Bake at 350° for 35-45 minutes, or until lightly browned.

Yield: 9 servings

Very close relative to best Betty!

APPLE CRUNCH

1   cup flour
1   cup brown sugar
3/4   cup quick oatmeal
1/2   cup (1 stick) butter or margarine, melted
2   cups apples, peeled and sliced

Mix together dry ingredients and melted butter until crumbly. Press 1/2 of mixture into a greased 9" x 9" square pan. Place sliced apples over mixture. Meanwhile, cook together the following sauce:

Sauce

1/2   cup sugar
2   T. cornstarch
1   cup water
2   T. butter or margarine
1/2   tsp. cinnamon
1   tsp. vanilla

Pour cooked sauce over apples. Sprinkle remainder of crumbs over top.
Bake at 350° for 45-50 minutes. Serve warm or cold.

Yield: 9 servings

APPLE COBBLER

1/2 cup brown sugar
2 T. cornstarch
1/2 tsp. cinnamon
1 1/4 cups water
1 T. lemon juice
1/2 tsp. grated lemon rind
6 cups apples, peeled and sliced
1 T. butter or margarine

In saucepan, combine brown sugar, cornstarch, cinnamon, lemon rind and juice, and water. Stir in sliced apples and cook until hot, about 10 minutes. Spoon into a 2 qt. casserole. Prepare topping for cobbler:

Cobbler Topping

1 cup flour
2 T. sugar
2 tsp. baking powder
1/4 tsp. salt
1/4 cup (1/2 stick) butter or margarine
1 egg, beaten
1/4 cup milk

1 T. sugar
1/4 tsp. cinnamon
1 T. butter or margarine

Sift together dry ingredients. Cut in butter. Mix egg with milk and add all at once to dry ingredients. Stir only enough to moisten all ingredients. Drop into mounds on hot apple mixture. Sprinkle with 1 T. sugar and 1/4 tsp. cinnamon. Dot with butter.
Bake at 425° for 20-30 minutes.

Yield: 6-8 servings

"The kids love this one"

OATMEAL APPLE CRUMBLE

4 cups apples, peeled and sliced
1/4 cup sugar
1 T. flour

3/4 cup brown sugar
1/2 cup flour
1 cup oatmeal
1/2 tsp. baking powder
1/2 tsp. cinnamon
1/4 tsp. nutmeg
1/2 cup (1 stick) butter or margarine, melted

Peel and slice apples and arrange in greased 9" x 9" baking pan. Combine 1/4 cup sugar and 1 T. flour and sprinkle over apples.

Mix together the brown sugar, flour, oatmeal, baking powder, spices, and melted butter. Sprinkle this crumbly mixture over apples.

Bake at 350° for 30-40 minutes, or until lightly browned.

Yield: 9 servings

Especially good warm with ice cream

APPLE DELIGHT

6 cups cooking apples, peeled and sliced
1/2 cup sugar

3/4 cup flour
3/4 cup sugar
1 tsp. baking powder
1/2 tsp. salt
1/2 tsp. cinnamon
1/4 tsp. allspice
1 egg, unbeaten
1/3 cup vegetable oil

Place sliced apples in lightly greased 9" x 9" square pan. Sprinkle sugar on top of apples.

Combine flour, sugar, baking powder, salt, and spices with egg and oil. Beat well. Spoon over top of apples.

Bake in 400° oven for 25-30 minutes, or until lightly browned.

Yield: 9 servings

APPLE PANDOWDY

4   cups apples, peeled and sliced
1/4   cup sugar
1/2   tsp. cinnamon
2   T. butter or margarine

1/2   cup sugar
1/2   cup (1 stick) butter or margarine
1   egg, beaten
1/2   cup flour
1/2   tsp. baking powder
1/4   tsp. salt
1   tsp. vanilla

Place sliced apples in buttered 9" x 9" baking pan or 2 qt. casserole. Sprinkle with cinnamon-sugar mixture. Dot with butter.

Cream sugar and butter. Add egg and beat well. Sift together flour, baking powder, and salt. Mix until mixture is well combined. Add vanilla and stir in. Drop by spoonfuls over apples and bake in 350° oven for 30-35 minutes, or until lightly browned. Serve warm or cold with ice cream, if desired.

Yield: 9 servings

QUICK APPLE DESSERT

4 large tart apples, peeled and sliced
1/2 cup orange juice
1/2 cup sugar
1/2 tsp. cinnamon

In ungreased 9" square pan, place the sliced apples. Pour orange juice over and sprinkle with sugar and cinnamon. Place the following crumb mixture over top:

Crumb Mixture

1 cup graham cracker crumbs
3 T. melted butter

Sprinkle this mixture over apples. Cover pan with foil.
Bake at 400° for 25-30 minutes, and uncover. Continue baking 5-10 more minutes.

Yield: 6-9 servings

JUICY APPLE DESSERT

2 eggs, beaten
1 cup sugar
4 cups apples, peeled and finely chopped
1/4 cup vegetable oil
2 cups flour
1 tsp. baking powder
1 tsp. salt
1 tsp. cinnamon
1/3 cup walnuts

Stir sugar into beaten eggs. Add chopped or grated apples and oil. Stir in sifted dry ingredients. Spread in greased 9" x 13" pan and bake at 350° for 35-40 minutes.

When done, poke holes in cake with fork and pour hot topping over cake. Cover pan with aluminum foil and let cool.

Topping

1/2 cup granulated sugar
1/2 cup brown sugar
2 T. flour
1/4 tsp. salt
2 cups water
1/2 cup (1 stick) butter or margarine
1 tsp. vanilla

Mix the sugars, flour, and salt in 1 qt. saucepan. Add water and cook for 3 minutes. Add butter and vanilla.

Yield: 16-20 servings

APPLE DESSERT

6 cooking apples, sliced
1/4 cup sugar
1/2 tsp. cinnamon
2 T. butter or margarine

1 cup flour
1/2 cup sugar
1 tsp. baking powder
1/2 tsp. salt
1/2 cup milk
2 T. butter or margarine

Slice apples into a greased 8" round pan. Sprinkle sugar and cinnamon over top. Dot with butter.

Sift together dry ingredients, cut in butter, and mix in the milk. Spoon over apples.

Bake at 350° for 30 minutes, or until lightly browned.

Yield: 6-8 servings

Almost as good as apple pie

APPLE TORTE

1   (1# 6   oz.) can apple pie filling
1   (1# 4   oz.) can crushed pineapple, undrained
1   pkg. yellow cake mix (2   layer size)
3/4   cup (1 1/2   stick) butter or margarine, melted
1   cup nuts

Spread apple pie filling in bottom of greased 9" x 13" pan. Layer undrained pineapple on top. Sprinkle dry cake mix over fruit. Drizzle melted butter over all. Sprinkle nuts on top. **Do not mix.**

Bake at 350° for 50-60 minutes. Serve plain or with ice cream or whipped cream.

Yield: 12-15 servings

DESSERT TOPPINGS

GINGERBREAD ALA MODE

Top gingerbread or unfrosted spice cake with a spoonful of applesauce and a scoop of butter brickle ice cream. Sprinkle cinnamon lightly on top, if desired.

PEANUT BRITTLE TOPPING
Fold 1/4 cup of crushed peanut brittle candy into 1 cup of lightly sweetened whipped cream or prepared whipped topping. Spoon on each serving of dessert or apple pie.

PRESERVES etc,

store by   the bushel

CARAMEL APPLES

6-8 medium apples
1 (14 oz.) pkg. caramels
3 T. water
6-8 wooden skewers

In double boiler, melt caramels with 3 T. water, stirring with wooden spoon until smooth. Wash and dry apples. Insert skewers in stem end and dip apples in caramel mixture covering all sides. Leave mixture over hot water while dipping. Place coated apples on wax paper.

Yield: 6-8 servings

DRIED APPLE TREATS

4 cooking apples, peeled
2 cups sugar
1/2 cup water

Combine sugar and water and boil until a rich syrup is formed. Cut apples into eights and add to boiling syrup. Let simmer until clear. Carefully spoon out apples, spread on cookie sheet. Let dry in sun 12 hours, turning once. Continue process for 2 or 3 more days.

Roll in sugar. Pack in plastic bag and refrigerate.

*Great after school snack,
or anytime snack*

APPLESAUCE

6-8 apples, peeled, cored and cut up
1/2 cup water
1/2 cup sugar

Add water to apples in saucepan. Cover and cook over low heat until apples are soft. Stir occasionally. Do not let apples scorch. Put through a food mill for a smooth applesauce or break up with a fork for a chunky applesauce. Stir in sugar and continue cooking until thickened.

Yield: Approximately 4 cups

Everyone should know how to make this!

APPLE BUTTER

10-12 medium apples
Water to cover
3 cups sugar
1 tsp. cinnamon
1/2 tsp. allspice

Wash apples and cut out blemishes. Quarter, leaving in skins and seeds. Place in large pan and cover with water. Cook over medium heat until fruit pulp is tender. Press through a food mill or sieve; discard peelings and seeds. Measure out 4 cups of fruit pulp; add sugar and spices. Bring to a boil over medium heat, stirring constantly. Reduce heat to simmer and cook until mixture is very thick and a deep reddish color. Pour into hot sterilized pint jars and seal. Process in boiling water bath 20 minutes.

Yield: Approximately 2 pints.

OLD WORLD SPICED APPLE BUTTER

4 cups apples, peeled and chopped
1/2 cup water or apple juice
3 cups sugar
1/4 cup vinegar
1 tsp. cinnamon
1/2 tsp. allspice
1/2 tsp. cloves
1/4 tsp. ginger

Cook apples in water or juice until tender, about 15 minutes. Mix in sugar, vinegar, and spices. Return to heat and continue simmering uncovered until mixture thickens. Pour into hot sterilized jars, leaving 1/2" headspace. Seal with jar lid. Process in boiling water bath 10 minutes.

Yield: Approximately 2 pints.

BRANDIED APPLE BUTTER

6 medium apples, peeled and quartered
1 orange, peeled and sliced
1 1/2 cups water
1 cup sugar
1/2 tsp. cinnamon
1/2 tsp. cloves
1/4 tsp. allspice
1/2 cup peach brandy

Mix together apples and orange in a saucepan and add water. Cover and cook over medium heat until fruit is tender, stirring occasionally. Press fruit through a food mill or sieve. Place fruit pulp back in pan; add sugar and spices and continue cooking until mixture is thick. Add peach brandy. Pack into hot sterilized jars and seal.

Yield: Approximately 2 half-pints.

Best if left to "ripen" for several months in a cool, dark place

APPLE JELLY

5# ripe tart apples or approximately 15 medium apples
5 cups water
9 cups sugar
1 box (1 3/4 oz.) powdered pectin

Wash apples, cutting out blemishes. Cut in small pieces without peeling or coring. The peel, seed, and core are high in pectin, which helps jelly 'jell." Can also add other apple peelings.

In large pan, cover apples with the water and boil gently, covered, for approximately 25 minutes, or until fruit is reduced to a soft pulp, stirring to crush apples. Then pour through a jelly bag and let drip. Do not squeeze. Measure out 7 cups of this apple juice and pour in large pan. Stir the pectin into apple juice. Place pan over high heat, stirring occasionally, until mixture comes to a full boil. Add sugar and bring to a full boil again, stirring constantly. Boil hard for 1 minute. Remove from heat. Skim off foam with metal spoon. Pour into sterilized jelly glasses or jars. Seal with melted paraffin.

Yield: Approximately 10-8 oz. glasses

QUICK APPLE JELLY

1 qt. bottled apple juice
1 box (1 3/4 oz.) powdered pectin
Few drops red food coloring
5 1/2 cups sugar

Pour apple juice in large pan; add pectin and food coloring to desired color. Bring to a full boil. Add sugar, stir, and return to boil. Boil hard for 2 minutes. Remove from heat and skim off foam. Pour into hot, sterilized jelly glasses and seal with melted paraffin.

Yield: Approximately 7 pints

OTHER VARIATIONS

Apple Cranberry Jelly. Use 2 cups apple juice and 2 cups cranberry juice to equal 1 qt. Proceed as above.

Red Hot Jelly. Add 1/3 cup red cinnamon hot candies with the sugar. (Omit red food coloring).

Apple-Mint Jelly. Substitute green food coloring for the red. After jelly has been poured into jelly jars, dip washed mint leaves and tender stems down into the hot jelly several times. Use 6-8 sprigs of mint for each pint.

FRUIT COMBO JAM

2　cups apples, chopped and cored, but unpeeled
3　cups raw cranberries
1 1/2　cups water
1 1/2　cups crushed pineapple, in own juice, undrained
2　T. lemon juice
4　cups sugar

Wash firm cranberries. Core and chop apples. Cook in water until fruit is tender. Press through a food mill or sieve. Measure out 3 cups of pulp and place in saucepan. Add crushed pineapple (with juice), lemon juice and sugar. Bring to a boil, stirring constantly. Reduce heat and cook until mixture is thick and transparent-about 10 minutes. Pour into hot sterilized jars and seal with metal rings and bands. Process in boiling water bath 10 minutes.

Yield: Approximately 2 pints.

APPLE AND PEACH PRESERVE

2　cups apples, peeled and cored
2　cups peaches
Juice of 2　lemons
3　cups sugar

Select firm, ripe peaches. Scald to remove peach skins. Chop apples and peaches into small pieces. Add lemon juice and sugar. Cook over medium heat until fruit is transparent and plump-about 20 minutes. Pour into hot sterilized jars and seal with melted paraffin.

Yield: Approximately 4-5 oz. glasses

FREEZING APPLES

Applesauce. Prepare applesauce same as recipe except increase amount of spices used by 1/4. Cool quickly and package in plastic containers or jars. Label and freeze at once.

Sliced Apples. Slice peeled apples into a salt brine solution of 2 T. salt to 1 qt. of water. Meanwhile, make sugar syrup by mixing 1 cup sugar to 2 cups water and simmer over low heat. Add 1/2 tsp. powdered ascorbic acid to syrup to prevent discoloration. Drain apples from brine solution and place in hot sugar syrup. Simmer for 3 minutes. Cool. Pack in jars, leaving 1/2" headspace. Seal and freeze.

Apples Pies.

Baked apples pies: Cool thoroughly and wrap for freezing. When ready to use, unwrap, and place frozen pie in 375° oven and bake for 30 minutes.

Unbaked apple pies: Prepare pie ready for baking. Do not slit top crust. Wrap and freeze. When ready to use, slit top crust, place frozen unbaked pie in 425° oven and bake for 20 minutes, reduce heat to 375° and bake for 30-40 minutes more.

INDEX

Images Unlimited
P.O. Box 305
Maryville, Missouri 64468

Please send _____ copies of **From the Apple Orchard—Recipes for Apple Lovers** at $10.95 each (Missouri residents add $.74 for each book). Enclose $2.00 shipping and handling charges for each book.

Enclosed is my check or money order for_____

Name _____

Street _____

City _____   State _____

ZIP _____

Make check payable to Images Unlimited.

- -

Images Unlimited
P.O. Box 305
Maryville, Missouri 64468

Please send _____ copies of **From the Apple Orchard—Recipes for Apple Lovers** at $10.95 each (Missouri residents add $.74 for each book). Enclose $2.00 shipping and handling charges for each book.

Enclosed is my check or money order for_____

Name _____

Street _____

City _____   State _____

ZIP _____

Make check payable to Images Unlimited.